P9-CAR-848

W 99

PENDING#:01008265B7502
PO#: EBERLE
CONF#:01008349K67C

CTN 1
OF 1

MIXED CARTON

SMP   PL#   1976 SEQ# 1717

005253818

UPS

Houghton Mifflin * 2700 N Richardt Ave
Indianapolis, IN 46219

SHIP TO: UNIV OF CONNECTICUT
PROF K EBERLE
ENGLISH DEPARTMENT
1 UNIVERSITY PLACE

STAMFORD CT 069012315

(420) SHIP TO POSTAL CODE

(420) 06901

UPS GROUND
TRACKING NUMBER

1Z 447 932 03 5253 8182

...ghton Mifflin Company   Boston   New York

Senior Sponsoring Editor: Mary Jo Southern
Senior Associate Editor: Ellen Darion
Editorial Assistant: Kate O'Sullivan
Senior Project Editor: Kathryn Dinovo
Senior Manufacturing Coordinator: Sally Culler
Senior Marketing Manager: Nancy Lyman

Cover design and image: Henry Rachlin

To Sharon

Printed in the U.S.A.

Library of Congress Catalog Card Number: 98-71998

ISBN: 0-395-91868-5

123456789-DH-02 01 00 99 98

As part of Houghton Mifflin's ongoing
commitment to the environment, this text
has been printed on recycled paper.

Contents

3 *Narration: Moving Through Time* 31

4 *Description: Moving Through Space and Time* 39

5 Exemplification: Writing with Examples 49

6 Analysis by Division: Examining the Parts 56

7 Process Analysis: Writing About Doing 63

8   *Cause and Effect: Determining Reasons and Outcomes*   *73*

9   *Classification: Establishing Groups*   *81*

Handbook *124*

Index   *147*

Preface

At a Glance: Paragraphs is the second-level book in the new *At a Glance* series of concise writing handbooks. Along with *At a Glance: Sentences* and *At a Glance: Essays*, it meets the current need for succinct, comprehensive, and up-to-date textbooks that students can afford. All three books provide basic instruction, exercises, and writing assignments at the designated level, as well as support material for instructors. *At a Glance: Sentences* and *At a Glance: Paragraphs* include a transition to the next level of writing while *At a Glance: Paragraphs* and *At a Glance: Essays* end with a Handbook, to which students can refer for help with sentence-level issues or for problems with mechanics. Each book in the *At a Glance* series can be used alone, as part of a two- or three-level sequence, or as a supplement to another type of textbook used in the course.

COMPREHENSIVE COVERAGE

Focusing on paragraph writing, *At a Glance: Paragraphs* begins with instruction in prewriting techniques, first-draft writing, revising, and editing—each phase illustrated with student examples. The book then presents ten patterns of paragraph writing, with a chapter devoted to each: narration, description, exemplification, analysis by division, process analysis, cause and effect, classification, comparison and contrast, definition, and argument.

The final chapter, "From Paragraph to Essay," provides a bridge to the writing of essays and includes examples and strategies for expanding paragraphs into short essays. *At a Glance: Paragraphs* concludes with a handbook that covers sentence-level issues (subjects and predicates, fragments, coordination and subordination, and so on); specific verb, pronoun, and modifier problems; punctuation; and capitalization.

INSTRUCTIONAL APPROACH

The instruction in *At a Glance: Paragraphs* is concise and direct, using thought-provoking example paragraphs, hands-on exercises, and writing practice for each rhetorical mode. Chapters 3 through 12 each present writing strategies for a particular paragraph pattern, followed by an annotated student example, a professional example with questions for students to answer, an exercise that gives students practice in organizing the pattern, topics (reading-related, career-related, and general) for writing such paragraphs, and a summary of guidelines specific to the pattern.

SUPPORT MATERIAL FOR INSTRUCTORS

- *Instructor's Guide.* Provides answers to exercises, a diagnostic test, a final test, and three quizzes for each major unit. Quizzes may be photocopied and distributed to students as additional classroom exercises.
- *English Microlab* for PC and Macintosh. Teaches and reinforces the basics of grammar, punctuation, and mechanics. An accompanying data disk allows instructors to manage and record group results.
- *Expressways,* Second Edition, for PC, Macintosh, and Windows. Interactive software that guides students as they write and revise paragraphs and essays.

ACKNOWLEDGMENTS

I am profoundly indebted to the following instructors who have reviewed this textbook: Marilyn Black, Middlesex Community College; Thomas Beverage, Coastal Carolina Community College; Deborah Burson-Smith, Southern University at New Orleans; David Lang, Golden Gate University; Phyllis MacCameron, Erie Community College; Kathy Masters, Arkansas State University; and Steve Stremmel, American River College. Thanks also to members of the English Department at Mt. San Antonio College, with special recognition to the Basic Courses Review Committee.

I deeply appreciate the work of freelance editor Marilyn Weissman as well as that of my colleagues at Houghton Mifflin: Mary Jo Southern, Ellen Darion, Kate O'Sullivan, Nancy Lyman, and Henry Rachlin.

For their cheerful, inspiring presence, I am especially grateful to my wife, my children and their spouses, and my grandchildren: Sharon, Kelly, Erin, Jeanne, Michael, Shane, Lauren, and Jarrett.

Lee Brandon

Student Overview

This book is designed to help you write better paragraphs. Chapters 1 and 2 focus on the writing process itself. You'll discover prewriting techniques to help you get started, and you'll learn ways to develop, revise, and edit your drafts until you produce a polished paragraph. Every stage is illustrated by the work of one student, whom we follow through the entire process.

Chapters 3 through 12 each describe a different pattern for developing an effective paragraph. Chapter 3, for example, is about narration; Chapter 4 is about description; Chapter 5 is about exemplification—that is, the use of examples. All chapters include a sample paragraph written by a student and one written by a professional writer. Throughout, questions and exercises help you put into practice what you have learned.

Chapter 13 discusses the essay in relationship to the paragraph and can help you expand some of your paragraphs into essays. After Chapter 13, you will find a Handbook, to which you can refer when you need assistance in grammar, usage, punctuation, and capitalization.

Following are some strategies you can follow to make the best use of this book and to jump-start the improvement in your writing skills.

1. **Be active and systematic in learning.** Take advantage of your instructor's expertise by being an active class member—one who takes notes, asks questions, and contributes to discussion. Become dedicated to systematic learning: determine your needs, decide what to do, and do it. Make learning a part of your everyday thinking and behavior.

2. **Read widely.** Samuel Johnson, a great English scholar, once said he didn't want to read anything by people who had written more than they had read. William Faulkner, a Nobel Prize winner in literature, said, "Read, read, read. Read everything—trash, classics, good and bad, and see how writers do it." Read to learn technique, to acquire ideas, to be stimulated to write. Especially read to satisfy your curiosity and to receive pleasure. If reading is a main component of your course, approach it as systematically as you do writing.

3. **Keep a journal.** Keeping a journal may not be required in your particular class, but whether required or not, jotting down your observations in a notebook is a good practice. Here are some topics for daily, or almost daily, journal writing:

- Summarize, evaluate, or react to reading assignments.
- Summarize, evaluate, or react to what you see on television and in movies, and to what you read in newspapers and in magazines.
- Describe and narrate situations or events you experience.
- Write about career-related matters you encounter in other courses or on the job.

Your journal entries may read like an intellectual diary, a record of what you are thinking about at certain times. Keeping a journal will help you to understand reading material better, to develop more language skills, and to think more clearly—as well as to become more confident and to write more easily so that writing becomes a comfortable, everyday activity. Your entries may also provide subject material for longer, more carefully crafted pieces. The most important thing is to get into the habit of writing something each day.

4. **Evaluate your writing skills.** Use the Self-Evaluation Chart inside the front cover of this book to list areas you need to work on. You can add to your lists throughout the entire term. Drawing on your instructor's comments, make notes on matters such as spelling, word choice, paragraph development, grammar, sentences, punctuation, and capitalization. As you master each problem area, you can check it off or cross it out.

Here is a partially filled out Self-Evaluation Chart, followed by some guidelines for filling out your own.

Self-Evaluation Chart

Spelling/ Word Choice	Paragraph Development	Grammar/ Sentences	Punctuation/ Capitalization
Separate	Topic	Fragment 127	Comma after long
A lot	sentence 1	Run-on 128	introductory
Studying	Use specific	Parallel	modifier 140
Boundary	examples 49	structure 130	Periods and
Avoid slang	Support 1	Subject-verb	commas inside
		agreement 136	quotation
			marks 142

Spelling/Word Choice: List words marked as incorrectly spelled on your assignments. Master the words on your list and add new words as you accumulate assignments. Also include new, useful words with their brief definitions and comments on word choice, such as avoiding slang, cliches, and vague or general words.

Paragraph Development: List suggestions your instructor made about writing strong topic sentences and attending to matters such as coherence, language, unity, emphasis, and support.

Grammar/Sentences: List problems such as subject-verb agreement, sentence fragments, comma splices, and run-ons. If you tend to begin sentences in the same way or to choose the same patterns, use your chart to remind yourself to vary your sentence patterns and beginnings.

Punctuation/Capitalization: List any problems you encounter with punctuation and capitalization. Because the items in this column may be covered in the Handbook at the end of this book, you can often use both rule numbers and page numbers for the references here.

5. **Be positive.** Most of the elements you record in your Self-Evaluation Chart probably are covered in *Paragraphs at a Glance.* The table of contents, the index, and the correction chart at the end of the book will direct you to the additional instruction you decide you need.

To improve your English skills, write with freedom, but revise and edit with rigor. Work with your instructor to set attainable goals, and proceed at a reasonable pace. Soon, seeing what you have mastered and checked off your list will give you a sense of accomplishment.

Finally, don't compare yourself with others. Compare yourself with yourself, and as you make progress, consider yourself what you are—a student on the path toward effective writing, a student on the path toward success.

1

The Paragraph and Prewriting

THE PARAGRAPH DEFINED

Paragraphs on a printed page are easy to spot because they are indented: each one starts with skipped spaces at the beginning of the first line. The kind of paragraph we will consider in this book contains three parts: the subject, the topic sentence, and the support.

The **subject** is what you will write about. That subject is likely to be broad and must be focused for more specific treatment. The **topic sentence** includes both the subject and the specific treatment of that subject. The treatment tells what you plan to *do* with the subject.

The topic sentence contains the central, or main, idea of the paragraph. Everything else in the paragraph supports the topic sentence: that is, all the other sentences explain or say more about the central idea. The **support** is the evidence or reasoning that explains the topic sentence. That support can be developed according to several basic patterns. Each pattern is the subject of one chapter of this book. A consideration of the questions below can help you choose the most appropriate pattern for your paragraph.

Narration: Can you illustrate your point by telling a story?
Description: How does something look, sound, feel, taste, or smell?
Exemplification: Can you support your main idea with examples of what you mean?
Analysis by division: What are the parts of a unit, and how do they work together?

1

Process analysis: How do you do something? How is (was) something done?

Cause and effect: What are the reasons for and/or results of an event, trend, or circumstance?

Classification: How can the ideas, persons, or things be grouped?

Comparison and contrast: How are two or more subjects similar and different?

Definition: What does a term mean?

Argument: What evidence and reasoning will convince someone that you are right?

The patterns above are often combined in writing. Whatever pattern or combination you use, however, the structure of the paragraph remains the same. A paragraph is a group of sentences, each with the function of supporting a single main idea, which is contained in the topic sentence. Here is a good example:

1   A cat's tail is a good barometer of its intentions. An excited or aggressively aroused cat will whip its entire tail back and forth. When I talk to Sam, he holds up his end of the conversation by occasionally flicking the tip of his tail. Mother cats move their tails back and forth to invite their kittens to play. A kitten raises its tail perpendicularly to beg for attention; older cats may do so to beg for food. When your cat holds its tail aloft while crisscrossing in front of you, it is trying to say, "Follow me"—usually to the kitchen, or more precisely, to the refrigerator. Unfortunately, many cats have lost their tails in refrigerator doors as a consequence.
—Michael W. Fox, "What Is Your Pet Trying to Tell You?"

The paragraph begins with the topic sentence: "A cat's tail is a good barometer of its intentions." The other sentences provide support for the topic sentence; they give examples to show that the topic sentence is true. The final sentence adds humor to the writing and gives a sense of ending or closure.

Although the topic sentence is often the first sentence of the paragraph, it does not have to be. Furthermore, the topic sentence is sometimes restated or echoed at the end of the paragraph, although again it does not have to be. However, a well-phrased concluding sentence can emphasize the central idea of the paragraph as well as provide a nice balance and ending.

A paragraph, however, is not a constraining formula: it has variations. In some instances, for example, the topic sentence is not found in a single sentence. It may be the combination of two sentences, or it may be an easily understood but unwritten underlying idea that unifies the paragraph. Nevertheless, the paragraph in most college writing contains discussion that supports a stated topic sentence, and the instruction in this book is based on that fundamental idea.

A SAMPLE PARAGRAPH

The following paragraph was written by college student Cyrus Norton. The subject of the paragraph and the treatment of the paragraph have been marked. Norton's topic sentence (not the first sentence in this case), his support of the topic sentence, and his concluding sentence are also marked.

This is the final draft. Following it, we will back up and, in this chapter and the next, show how Norton moved during the writing process from his initial idea to this polished paragraph.

Magic Johnson, an NBA Great

Cyrus Norton

Some NBA (National Basketball

Association) players are good because they

Topic sentence   have a special talent in one area. Magic

Johnson was a great NBA star because he was

excellent in shooting, passing, rebounding,

Support for shooting   and leading. As a shooter few have ever

equaled him. He could slam, shovel, hook, and

fire from three-point range—all with deadly

accuracy. As for free throws, he led all NBA

players in shooting percentage in 1988-89.

Support for passing   While averaging more than twenty points per

game, he helped others become stars with his

passes. As the point guard (the quarterback of basketball), he was always near the top in the league in assists and was famous for his "no-look" pass, which often surprised even his teammates with its precision. When he wasn't shooting or passing, he was

Support for rebounding   rebounding. A top rebounding guard is unusual in professional basketball, but Magic, at six feet, nine inches, could bump shoulders and leap with anyone. These three qualities made him probably the most spectacular triple-double threat of all time. "Triple-double" means reaching two digits in scoring, assists, and rebounding. Magic didn't need more for greatness in the NBA, but he had more. With his everlasting smile and

Support for leading   boundless energy, he was also an inspirational team leader. He always believed in himself and his team. When his team was down by a point and three seconds remained on the game clock, the fans looked for Magic to get the ball. They watched as he dribbled once, he faded, he leaped, he twisted, and he hooked one in from twenty feet! That was

Concluding sentence   magic. That was Magic.

Let's consider Norton's paragraph in light of what we know about paragraphs in general. Magic Johnson, the subject, is what the paragraph is all about. In this example, the title also names the subject. The topic sentence, the unifying and controlling idea, makes a clear statement about what the writer will do with the subject. As usual, the topic sentence appears near the beginning of the paragraph. The support gives evidence and examples to back up the controlling idea. And the last sentence, "That was Magic!" echoes the topic sentence. It is usually called the concluding sentence.

The author has told you what he was going to say, he has said it, and finally he has reminded you of what he has told you. The concluding sentence is sometimes omitted. The two most common designs of paragraphs in college writing are these:

> topic sentence→support→concluding sentence
> topic sentence→support

"Magic Johnson, an NBA Great" is a typical paragraph: a group of sentences that present and develop an idea. In college writing a paragraph is usually expository; that is, its purpose is to explain. In this example, you, the reader, get the point. You're informed, and maybe even entertained a little by the explanation.

If you follow certain principles and then practice, practice, practice, you too can write effective paragraphs. Success lies in following directions and using the right set of tools. And the more times you use those basic directions and tools, the better you'll get. Eventually, you will be able to complete your task skillfully, hardly thinking about what you're doing.

Principles at a Glance

Paragraph: A group of sentences that present and develop an idea.

Topic sentence: The sentence that expresses the controlling idea of the paragraph. The topic sentence mentions the subject (what the paragraph is about) and the treatment (what the writer will do with the subject).

Support: Evidence such as details, examples, and explanations that back up the topic sentence.

Basic paragraph designs:
Topic sentence→support→concluding sentence
Topic sentence→support

THE WRITING PROCESS: PREWRITING

There are easy, comfortable, and effective ways to write a paragraph. Writing does not mean merely putting words on paper. It is a process that often involves several steps: using prewriting techniques to explore a topic, limiting and then developing the topic, making an outline, writing a draft, revising the draft as often as necessary, and editing. At times, writers discover that their topic sentence or their outline does not work, and they go back and alter their original concept or design.

The Blank Sheet of Opportunity

Certain strategies commonly grouped under the heading *prewriting* can help you get started and develop your ideas. Actually, these strategies—freewriting, brainstorming, clustering, defining a topic, and outlining—are very much a part of writing. The understandable desire to skip to the finished statement is what causes the most common student-writer grief: that of not filling the blank sheet or of filling it but not significantly improving upon the blankness. The prewriting strategies that follow will help you attack the blank sheet constructively with imaginative thought, analysis, and experimentation. They can lead to clear, effective communication.

Although the strategies can work very well, you do not need to use all of them in all writing assignments. Learn them now, and use them when they are needed. Think of this approach as carrying a box of tools and then selecting the ones that do the job.

Freewriting

One strategy is **freewriting,** an exercise that its originator, Peter Elbow, has called "babbling in print." In freewriting, you write without stopping, letting your ideas tumble forth. You do not concern yourself with the fundamentals of writing, such as punctuation and spelling. Freewriting is an adventure into your memory and imagination. It is concerned with discovery, invention, and exploration. If you are at a loss for words on your subject, write in a comment such as "I don't know what is coming next" or "blah, blah, blah," and continue when relevant words come. The important thing is not to stop writing. Freewriting immediately eliminates the blank page and thereby helps you break through an emotional barrier, but that is not the only benefit. The words that you sort through in that idea kit will include some you can use. You can then underline or circle those words, and even add notes on the side so that the freewriting continues to grow even after its initial spontaneous expression.

The way in which you proceed depends on the type of assignment:

working with a topic of your choice,
working from a restricted list of topics, or
working with a prescribed topic.

The *topic of your choice* affords you the greatest freedom of exploration. You would probably select a subject that interests you and freewrite about it, allowing your mind to wander among its many parts, perhaps mixing fact and fantasy, direct experience, and hearsay. A freewriting about music might uncover areas of special interest and knowledge, such as jazz or folk rock, that you would want to pursue further in freewriting or other prewriting strategies.

Working from a *restricted list* requires a more focused freewriting. With the list, you can, of course, experiment with several topics to discover what is most suitable for you. If, for example, "career choice," "career preparation," "career guidance," and "career prospects" are on the restricted list, you would probably select one and freewrite about it. If it works well for you, you would probably proceed with the next step of your prewriting. If you are not satisfied with what you uncover in freewriting, you would explore another item from the restricted list.

When working with a *prescribed topic,* you focus on a particular topic and try to restrict your freewriting to its boundaries. If your topic specifies a division of a subject area such as "political involvement of your generation," then you would tie those key words to your own information, critical thinking, and imaginative responses. If the topic is restricted to, let's say, a particular reading selection such as your reactions to a poem, then that poem would give you the framework for your free associations with your own experiences, creations, and opinions.

You should learn to use freewriting because it will often serve you well, but you need not use it every time you write. Some very short writing assignments do not call for freewriting. An in-class assignment may not allow time for freewriting.

Nevertheless, freewriting is often a useful strategy in your toolbox of techniques. It can help you get words on paper, break emotional barriers, generate topics, develop new insights, and explore ideas.

Freewriting can lead to other stages of prewriting and writing, and it can also provide content as you develop your topic.

The following example of freewriting, and the writing, revising, and editing examples in Chapter 2, are from student Cyrus Norton's work on "Magic Johnson, an NBA Great" (p. 3). Norton's topic came from a restricted list; he was directed to write about the success of an individual. Had he been working with a prescribed topic, he might have been directed to concentrate on a specific aspect of Johnson's career, such as business, philanthropy, public service, or the one Norton chose: great basketball playing.

Sample Freewriting

great	`Magic Johnson was the `<u>`greatest`</u>` player`
	`I've ever seen in professional basketball.`
leader	`Actually not just a player but a `<u>`leader`</u>` and`
inspiration	`an `<u>`inspiration`</u>` to the team so they always`
	`gave him the ball when the game was on the`
	`line. It was too bad his career was cut short`
	`when they discovered he was HIV positive.`
	`Actually he came back but then retired again.`
rich	`He made `<u>`a lot of money`</u>` and I guess he`
	`invested it wisely because his name is linked`
	`to the Lakers and theaters and more. Also to`
	`programs making people aware of the danger of`
	`AIDS and helping kids grow up and stay out of`
	`trouble. But the main thing about Magic is`
playing	`the `<u>`way he played`</u>`. He could do everything. He`
	`even played center one time in a championship`
scoring	`game. He always `<u>`scored a lot`</u>` and he could`
pass	<u>`pass`</u>` like nobody else. Even though he was a`
rebound	`guard, he was tall and could `<u>`rebound`</u>`. He was`
	`great. Everyone says so.`

After doing this freewriting, Cyrus Norton went back through his work looking for ideas that might be developed in a paper.

Observe how he returned to his freewriting and examined it for possible ideas to develop for a writing assignment. As he recognized those ideas, he underlined key words and phrases and made a few notes in the margins. By reading only the underlined words, you can obtain a basic understanding of what is important to him. It is not necessary to underline entire sentences.

In addition to putting some words on that dreaded blank sheet of paper, he discovered that he had quite a lot of information about Magic Johnson and that he had selected a favorable topic to develop. The entire process took little time. Had he found few or no promising ideas, he might have freewritten about another topic. In going back through his work, he saw some errors in writing, but he did not correct them, because the purpose of freewriting is discovery, not correct grammar, punctuation, or spelling. He was confident that he could then continue with the process of writing a paper.

Brainstorming

This prewriting strategy features key words and phrases that relate in various ways to the subject area or to the specific topic you are concerned with. One effective way to get started is to ask the "big six questions" about your subject area: Who? What? Where? When? Why? and How? Then let your mind run free as you jot down answers in single entries or lists. Some of the big six questions may not fit, and some may be more important than others, depending on the purposes of your writing. For example, if you were writing about the causes of a situation, the Why? question could be more important than the others; if you were concerned with how to do something, the How? question would predominate. If you were writing in response to a reading selection, you would confine your thinking to questions appropriately related to the content of that reading selection.

Whatever your focus for the questions is, the result is likely to be numerous ideas that will provide information for continued exploration and development of your topic. Thus your pool of information for writing widens and deepens.

An alternative to the big six questions approach is simply to make a list of words and phrases related to your subject area or specific topic.

Cyrus Norton continued with the topic of Magic Johnson, and his topic tightened to focus on particular areas. Although he could have listed the annotations and the words he underlined in his freewriting, he used the big six questions for his framework.

Who: Magic Johnson
What: great basketball player
Where: the NBA

When: for more than ten years
Why: love of game and great talent
How: shooting, passing, rebounding, leading, coolness, in-
   spiring

As it turned out, How? was the most fruitful question for Norton, and it led him to a list.

Clustering

Still another prewriting technique is *clustering* (also called *map-*
ping). Start by "double bubbling" your topic. That is, write it down
in the middle of the page and draw a double circle around it. Then
respond to the question "What comes to mind?" Single-bubble
other ideas on spokes radiating out from the hub that contains the
topic. Any bubble can lead to another bubble or numerous bubbles
in the same way. This strategy is sometimes used instead of or before making an outline to organize and develop ideas.

The more specific the topic inside the double bubble, the fewer
the number of spokes that will radiate with single bubbles. For example, a topic such as "high school dropouts" would have more
spokes than "reasons for dropping out of high school."

Here is Cyrus Norton's cluster on the subject of Magic Johnson.

THE TOPIC SENTENCE

The topic sentence is the most important sentence in your prewriting and also in your paragraph. It includes two parts: the subject and the treatment, what you will do with your subject. Consider, for example, this topic sentence:

Magic Johnson was a great all-around NBA player.
    subject   treatment

It is an effective topic sentence because it limits the subject and indicates treatment that can be developed in additional sentences. Another sound version is the following, which goes further to include divisions for the treatment.

Magic Johnson was a great NBA star because he was excellent in
    subject   treatment
shooting, passing, rebounding, and leading.

Ineffective topic sentences are often too broad, vague, or narrow.

INEFFECTIVE: TOO BROAD OR VAGUE	Magic Johnson was everything to everybody. Magic Johnson was fun. Magic Johnson was a success in basketball.
INEFFECTIVE: TOO NARROW	Magic Johnson went to the University of Michigan. Magic Johnson signed with the Los Angeles Lakers.

Usually, simple statements of fact do not need or do not allow for development.

EXERCISE 1

Mark the following statements for subject (S) and treatment (T), and label each as E (effective), or, I (ineffective). The effective ones are those that you can easily relate to supporting evidence. The ineffective statements are too broad, too vague, or too narrowly factual.

_____ 1. Columbus is located in Ohio.

_____ 2. Columbus is a fabulous city.

_____ 3. Columbus has dealt thoroughly with its housing problems.

_____   4. A monkey is a primate.

_____   5. Monkeys are fun.

_____   6. In clinical studies monkeys have demonstrated a remarkable ability to reason.

_____   7. More than a million cats are born in California each year.

_____   8. A simple observation of a domesticated cat in the pursuit of game will show that it has not lost its instinct for survival.

_____   9. The two teams in the Rose Bowl have similar records.

_____   10. Michigan State is in the Rose Bowl.

EXERCISE 2

Complete the following entries by making each into a solid topic sentence. Only a subject and part of the treatment are provided. The missing part may be more than a single word.

EXAMPLE: Car salespersons behave differently depending on <u>the car they are selling and the kind of customer they are serving.</u>

1. Television commercials are often _____

   _____

2. Rap music promotes _____

   _____

3. My part-time job taught me _____

   _____

4. I promote environmental conservation by _____

   _____

5. The clothing that a person wears often reveals _____

   _____

6. My close friend is preoccupied with _____

_____

7. Winning a lot of money is not always _____

_____

8. Country music appeals to our most basic _____

_____

9. Friendship depends on _____

_____

10. A good salesperson should _____.

_____

EXERCISE 3

Make each of the following subjects into a topic sentence.

1. Computer literacy

_____

_____

_____

2. My taste in music

_____

_____

_____

3. Bus transportation

_____

_____

_____

4. The fear of crime

_____

_____

_____

5. An excellent boss

_____

_____

_____

6. Doing well in college English classes

_____

_____

_____

7. Violence on television

_____

_____

_____

8. Daycare centers

_____

_____

_____

9. Good health

_____

_____

_____

10. Teenage voters

_____

_____

_____

OUTLINES

An outline is a pattern for showing the relationship of ideas. The two main outline forms are the *sentence outline* (each entry is a complete sentence) and the *topic outline* (each entry is a key word or phrase). The topic outline is commonly used for paragraphs.

Indentation, number and letter sequences, punctuation, and the placement of words are important to clear communication. We do not read an outline expecting to be surprised by form and content, as we do a poem. We go to the outline for information, and we expect to find ideas easily. Unconventional marks (circles, squares, half-parentheses) and items out of order are distracting and, therefore, undesirable in an outline. The standard form is as easily mastered as a nonstandard form, and it is worth your time to learn it. Outlining is not difficult: the pattern is flexible and can have any number of levels and parts.

Basically, an outline shows how a topic sentence is supported. Thus it shows the organization of the paragraph. The most important supporting material, called the major support, is indicated by Roman numerals. That major support is developed by less important supporting material, called the minor support, which in turn may be developed by details and/or examples. Here is the outline developed by Cyrus Norton:

TOPIC SENTENCE: Magic Johnson was a great NBA star because he was excellent in shooting, passing, rebounding, and leading.

I. Shooting (major support)
  A. Short shots (minor support)
    1. Shovel (detail)
    2. Slam-dunk (detail)
  B. Long shots (minor support)
  C. Free throws (minor support)
II. Passing (major support)
  A. No-look (minor support)
  B. Precise (minor support)
III. Rebounding (major support)
  A. Leaping (minor support)
  B. Bumping shoulders (minor support)
IV. Leading (major support)
  A. Energy (minor support)
  B. Spirit (minor support)
    1. Faith (detail)
    2. Smile (detail)

The foundation of a good outline and hence a good paragraph is a strong topic sentence, which means one with a specific subject and a well-defined treatment. After writing a good topic sentence, the next step is to divide the treatment into parts. Just what the parts are will depend on what you are trying to do in the treatment. Consider the thought process involved. What sections of material would be appropriate in your discussion to support or explain that topic sentence?

Among the most common forms of division are these:

Divisions of time or incident to tell a story

    I. Situation
   II. Conflict
 III. Struggle
 IV. Outcome
   V. Meaning

Divisions of example or examples

    I. First example
  II. Second example
 III. Third example (or divide one example into three or more aspects)

Divisions of causes or effects

    I. Cause (or effect) one
  II. Cause (or effect) two
 III. Cause (or effect) three

Divisions of a unit into parts (such as the federal government into executive, legislative, and judicial branches—or Magic Johnson's all-around skill into shooting, passing, rebounding, and leading)

    I. Part one
  II. Part two
 III. Part three

Divisions of how to do something or how something was done

    I. Preparations
  II. Steps
    A. Step 1
    B. Step 2
    C. Step 3

Fill in the missing parts. Considering whether you are dealing with time, examples, causes, effects, parts, or steps may be useful. The answers will vary depending on your individual experiences and views.

1. Too many of us are preoccupied with material things.

    I. Clothing

    II. Cars

    III. _____

2. Television sit-coms may vary, but every successful show has certain components.

    I. Good acting

    II. _____

    III. Good situations

    IV. _____

3. A female who is trying to discourage unwanted sexual advances should take several measures.

    I. _____

    II. Set clear boundaries

    III. Avoid compromising situations

4. Concentrating during reading involves various techniques.

    I. Preview material

    II. Pose questions

    III. _____

5. Crime has some bad effects on a nearby neighborhood.

    I. People fearful

        A. Don't go out at night

        B. _____

    II. People without love for neighborhood

        A. _____

        B. Put houses up for sale

    III. People as victims

        A. Loss of possessions

        B. _____

6. Exercising can improve a person's life.

    I. Looks better

        A. Skin

        B. _____

    II. Feels better

        A. _____

        B. Body

    III. Performs better

        A. Work

        B. _____

7. Shoppers in department stores can be grouped according to needs.

    I. _____

    II. Special-needs shoppers

    III. Bargain hunters

8. There are different kinds of intelligence based on situations.

    I. Street-smart

    II. Common sense

    III. _____

9. Smoking should be discouraged.

    I. Harm to smokers

        A. _____

        B. Cancer risk

    II. Harm to those around smokers

        A. _____

        B. Fellow workers

   III. Cost

   A. Industry—production and absenteeism

   B. _____

10. An excellent police officer must have six qualities.

   I. _____

   II. Knowledge of law

   III. _____

   IV. Emotional soundness

   V. Skill in using weapons

   VI. _____

WRITER'S GUIDELINES AT A GLANCE: THE PARAGRAPH AND PREWRITING

1. A paragraph is a group of sentences, each with the function of stating or supporting a single controlling idea that is contained in the topic sentence.
2. A paragraph contains two parts: the topic sentence and the support.

   - The topic sentence expresses the controlling idea of the paragraph. It has a subject (what the paragraph is about) and indicates the treatment (what the writer will do with the subject).
   - The support is the evidence, such as details, examples, and explanations, that backs up the topic sentence.

3. The two most common paragraph designs in college writing are these:

   - Topic sentence→support→concluding sentence
   - Topic sentence→support

4. Prewriting includes activities you do before writing your first draft or whenever you need new ideas.

   - *Freewriting:* writing without stopping, letting your ideas tumble forth. Freewriting helps you break emotional barriers, generate topics, and discover and explore ideas.
   - *Brainstorming:* a listing procedure that helps you discover key words and phrases that relate to your topic. Begin by asking

Who? What? Where? When? Why? and How? questions of your topic.

- *Clustering:* a graphic way of showing connections and relationships. Start by "double-bubbling" your topic. Then ask "What comes to mind?" and single-bubble other ideas on spokes radiating out from the double bubble.

- *Outlining:* a form for indicating the relationship of ideas. An outline shows how a topic sentence is supported. Thus it reveals the organization of the paragraph. Major support is indicated by Roman numerals. The major support is developed by minor support, which in turn may be developed by details and/or examples.

Topic sentence
I. Major support
   A. Minor support
   B. Minor support
     1. Details and/or examples
     2. Details and/or examples
II. Major support
   A. Minor support
   B. Minor support

2

Writing, Revising, and Editing the Paragraph

WRITING YOUR FIRST DRAFT

Once you have completed your topic sentence and outline (or list or cluster), you are ready to begin writing your paragraph. The initial writing is called the first, or rough, draft. Your topic sentence is likely to be at or near the beginning of your paragraph and will be followed by your support as ordered by your outline.

Paying close attention to your outline for basic organization, you should proceed without worrying about the refinements of writing. This is not the time to concern yourself with perfect spelling, grammar, or punctuation. After you have finished that first draft, take a close look at it. If your topic sentence is sound and your outline has served you well, you have a basic discussion. You have made a statement and supported it.

Don't be embarrassed by the roughness of your work. You should be embarrassed only if you leave it that way. You are seeing the reason why a first draft is called "rough." Famous authors have said publicly that they wouldn't show their rough drafts even to their closest, most forgiving friends.

The Recursive Factor

The process of writing can be called recursive, which means "going back and forth." In this respect, writing is like reading. If you do not understand what you have read, you back up and read it again. After you have reread a passage, you may still need to read it selectively. The same can be said of writing. If, for example, after having developed an outline and started writing your first draft, you discover

21

that your subject is too broad, you have to back up, narrow your topic sentence, and then adjust your outline. You may even want to return to an early cluster of ideas to see how you can use a smaller grouping of them. Revision is usually the most recursive of all parts of the writing process. You will go over your material again and again until you are satisfied that you have expressed yourself as well as you possibly can.

REVISING YOUR WRITING

The term *first draft* suggests quite accurately that there will be other drafts, or versions, of your writing. Only in the most dire situations, such as an in-class examination when you have time for only one draft, should you be satisfied with a single effort.

What you do beyond the first draft is revising and editing. Revision concerns itself with organization, content, and language effectiveness. Editing involves a final correcting of mistakes in spelling, punctuation, and capitalization. In practice, editing and revision are not always separate activities, though writers usually wait until the next-to-the-last draft to edit some minor details and attend to other small points that can be easily overlooked.

Successful revision almost always involves intense, systematic rewriting. You should learn to look for certain aspects of skillful writing as you enrich and repair your first draft. To help you recall these aspects so that you can keep them in mind and examine your material in a comprehensive fashion, this textbook offers a memory device—an acronym in which each letter suggests an important feature of good writing and revision. This device enables you to memorize the features of good writing quickly. Soon you will be able to recall and refer to them automatically. These features need not be attended to individually when you revise your writing, though they may be. And they need not be attended to in the order presented here. The acronym is CLUESS (pronounced "clues"), which provides this guide:

Coherence
Language
Unity
Emphasis
Support
Sentences

Coherence

Coherence is the flow of ideas, with each idea leading logically and smoothly to the next. It is achieved by numbering parts or otherwise indicating time (*first, second, third, then, next, soon,* and so on), giving directions (according to space, as in "To the right is a map, and to the left of that map is a bulletin board"), using transitional words (*however, otherwise, therefore, similarly, hence, on the other hand, then, consequently, accordingly, thus*), using demonstrative pronouns (*this, that, those*), and moving in a clear order (from the least important to the most important or from the most important to the least important).

Language

Language here means using words that are suitable for what you are writing and for your audience. In college writing that means you will usually avoid slang and clichés such as "a barrel of laughs," "happy as a clam," and "six of one and a half dozen of another." Your writing will contain standard grammar and usage.

Unity

Unity begins with a good topic sentence. Everything in your paragraph should be related and subordinated to your topic sentence. Repetition of a key word or phrase can make the unity even stronger.

Emphasis

Emphasize important ideas by using *position* (the most emphatic parts of a work are the beginning and the end), *repetition* (repeat key words and phrases), and *isolation* (a short, direct sentence among longer ones will usually command attention).

Support

Support is the material that backs up, justifies, or proves your topic sentence. Work carefully with the material from your outline (or list or cluster) to make sure that your ideas are well supported. If your paragraph is skimpy and your ideas slender, you are probably generalizing and not explaining how you arrived at your conclusions. Avoid repetition that does not add to the content; use details and examples; indicate parts and discuss relationships; explain why your generalizations are true, logical, and accurate. Your reader can't accept your ideas unless he or she knows by what reasoning or use of evidence you developed them.

Sentences

Be sure your sentences are complete (not fragments) and that you have not incorrectly combined word groups that could be sentences (comma splices and run-ons). Consider using different types of sentences and different sentence beginnings.

Write as many drafts as necessary, revising as you go for all the aspects of effective writing. Don't confuse revising with editing (the final stage of the writing process); don't get bogged down in fixing such things as spelling and punctuation.

EDITING YOUR WRITING

This final stage of the writing process involves a careful examination of your work. Look for problems with capitalization, omissions, punctuation, and spelling (COPS).

Before you submit your writing to your instructor, do what almost all professional writers do before sending their material along: read it aloud, to yourself or to a willing accomplice. Reading material aloud will help you catch any awkwardness of expression, omission and misplacement of words, and other problems that are easily overlooked by an author.

As you can see, writing is a process and is not a matter of just sitting down and "banging out" a statement. The parts of the process from prewriting to revising to editing are connected, and your movement is ultimately forward, but this process allows you to go back and forth in the recursive manner discussed earlier. If your outline is not working, perhaps the flaw is in your topic sentence. You may need to go back and fix it. If one section of your paragraph is skimpy, perhaps you will have to go back and reconsider the pertinent material in your outline or clustering. There you might find more details or alter a statement so that you can move into more fertile areas of thought.

Cyrus Norton wrote this first draft, marked it for revision, and then completed the final draft, which you read on page 3. For simplification, only this draft is shown, though a typical paper might include several drafts, including one on which the author has done nothing but edit his or her revised writing.

Magic Johnson ⋏ an NBA Great ⋏

(National Basketball Association)
Some NBA ⋏players are good because they
have a special talent
~~are good~~ in one area ⋏ ~~such as shooting,~~

~~passing, or rebounding.~~ Magic Johnson was a ⋏
        NBA star   excellent   shooting, passing,
great ⋏because he was ~~good~~ in ~~all of those~~
rebounding, and leading
~~things and more~~. As a shooter few have ~~been~~
ever equaled him
~~able to do what he could~~. He could slam,

shovel, hook, and fire from three-point
        ⍏—all with deadly accuracy   As for
ran⋏ge. ~~When it came to~~ free throws, he led

all NBA players in shooting percentage in
                    While
1988-89. ~~Then~~ he averaged more than twenty

points per game, he helped others become
with his passes.   (the quarterback of basketball) ⋏
stars. As the point guard he was always near
                    s
the top in the league in a⋏sists and was

famous for his "no-look" passe~~s~~ ⋏Which often
                                its
surprised even his teammates with ~~their~~
When he wasn't shooting or passing he was rebounding.
precision. A top rebounding guard is unusual,

but Magic, ~~standing~~ at six feet nine inches
                    u
tall, could bump sho⋏lders and jump with

anyone. These three qualities made him

probably the most spectacular triple-double

"Triple-double" means reaching two digits in scoring, assists, and rebounding.

threat of all time. Magic didn't need more

for greatness in the NBA, but he had more. He

was also an inspirational team leader with

his everlasting smile and boundless energy.

He   ed
Always believing in himself and his team.

When his team was down by a point and three

remained on the game clock   the fans
seconds were left, you always looked for

                                    They
Magic to get the ball. Then you watched as he

            he   he   he
dribbled once, faded, leaped, twisted, and

he   , That was magic.
hooked one in from twenty feet That was

Magic.

▌ EXERCISE 1

Treat the following paragraph as your own rough draft, and mark it
in the way Cyrus Norton marked *his* rough draft. First consider *co*-
herence, *l*anguage, *u*nity, *e*mphasis, *s*upport, and *s*entences
(CLUESS). Then edit it, correcting fundamentals such as *c*apitalization, *o*missions, *p*unctuation, and *s*pelling (COPS).

High school dress codes don't make any sense to me.

I've heard all the reasons. Too many kids wear gang

clothes and some get attacked or even killed. Parents

have to put up too much money and even then the kids

without parents with deep pockets can't compete. And then

there are those that say kids behave bad if they dress in

a free spirit way. Let's take them one at a time. As for

the gang stuff, it's mainly how you act, not how you

look, and if the gang stuff is still a problem, then just ban certain items of clothing. You don't have to go to the extreames of uniforms, just change the attitude, not the clothes. Then comes the money angle. Let the kid get a part-time job if they want better clothes. The behavior number is not what I can relate to. I mean, you go to class and learn, and you do it the school way, but the way you dress should have something to do with how you want to express yourself. Do they want to turn out a bunch of little robots that think the same way, behave the same way, and yes with the dress code even look the same way. Get real! If they'll cut us some slack with how we dress, they'll get happier campers in the classroom. Later better-citizens in society.

▌ EXERCISE 2

Mark this rough draft for *c*oherence, *l*anguage, *u*nity, *e*mphasis, *s*upport, and *s*entences (CLUESS). Then edit it, correcting fundamentals such as *c*apitalization, *o*missions, *p*unctuation, and *s*pelling (COPS).

Young voters are not voting the way they should. The latest figures show that only twenty percent are going to the poles. The next older generation is, the so-called baby boomers, they are going to the poles at about twice that rate. Since I'm part of the young group, I'm concerned, but the answers to why we usually don't bother to vote are as obvious as the nose on your face. For one thing the younger people don't think that voting changes anything. The political parties are all about the same and the candidates look and talk alike, even though they seem angry with each other. For another a lot of young voters don't have parents that voted or even talked about politics when they were growing up, they don't either. Still another thing is that the issues going around don't move young people that much. The politicians talk about the national debt and social security and health care and we're concerned about jobs and the high cost of education. If they could get people we could believe in and they would talk about issue that matter to us, then maybe they'd see more of us at the polls.

EXERCISE 3

Mark the following rough draft for coherence, language, unity, emphasis, support, and sentences (CLUESS). Then edit it, correcting fundamentals such as capitalization, omissions, punctuation, and spelling (COPS).

Make me a traffic cop, and I'll crack down on certain types of driver. First off are the drunks. I'd zap them off the highways right off, and any cop would. But what I'm really talking about is the jerks of the highway. Near the top are the up-tight lane changers, for example, this morning when I was driving to school, I saw several. I could have carved at least a couple notches in a vilation pad, and I wasn't even cranky. They cut off people and force their way in, and leave behind upset and hurt people. Then there's the left-turn bullies the ones that keep moving out when the yellow turn to red. They come in all ages and sexes, they can be young or old,

male or female. Yesterday, I saw this female in a pick-up
barrel right out into the teeth of a red light. She had a
baby on board. She had lead in her foot. She had evil in
her eye. She was hostile and self-centered. Taking
advantage of others. She knew that the facing traffic
would probably not pull out and risk a head-on crash. The
key word there is probably but many times people with a
green light do move out and colide with the left turn
bullies. Third, I'd sap the tailgaters. No one goes fast
enough for these guys. I'm not alone in this peeve. One
bumper sticker reads, "Stay back. I chew tobacky." And
James Bond sprayed oil on cars that chased him. Since the
first is dirty and the second is against the law, if I
had the clout of a Rambo-cop I'd just rack up a lot of
tailgater tickets. But there's a lot of road demons out
there. Maybe it's good I'm not a traffic cop, Rambo or
otherwise, cause traffic cops are suppose to inforce
hundreds of laws. I don't know if I'd have time cause I
have my own pet peeves in mind.

EXERCISE 4

Fill in the two blanks below to complete the topic sentence.

_____ [person's name] is an excellent _____
[boss, coach, doctor, neighbor, parent, preacher, teacher, sibling].

Then use the topic sentence for a paragraph. Go through the complete writing process. Use one or more prewriting techniques
(freewriting, brainstorming, clustering, outlining), write a first
draft, revise your draft as many times as necessary, edit your work,
and write a final polished paragraph.

In your drafts, you may rephrase the topic sentence as necessary. Using the paragraph on pages 3–4 as a model (showing Magic Johnson as a shooter, passer, rebounder, and leader), divide your topic into whatever qualities make your subject an excellent example of whichever type of person you have chosen.

WRITER'S GUIDELINES AT A GLANCE: WRITING, REVISING, EDITING

1. **Writing the rough draft:** Referring to your outline for guidance and to your topic sentence for limits, write a first, or rough, draft. Do not get caught up in correcting and polishing your writing during this stage.
2. **Revising:** Mark and revise your rough draft, rewriting as many times as necessary to produce an effective paragraph. The main points of revision are contained in the acronym CLUESS, expressed here as questions.

> Coherence: Does the material flow smoothly, with each idea leading logically to the next?
>
> Language: Are the words appropriate for the message, occasion, and audience?
>
> Unity: Are all ideas related to and subordinate to the topic sentence?
>
> Emphasis: Have you used techniques such as repetition and placement of ideas to emphasize your main point(s)?
>
> Support: Have you presented material to back up, justify, or prove your topic sentence?
>
> Sentences: Have you used some variety of structure and avoided fragments, comma splices, and run-ons?

3. **Editing:** Examine your work carefully. Look for problems in capitalization, omissions, punctuation, and spelling (COPS).

3

Narration: Moving Through Time

WRITING NARRATIVE PARAGRAPHS

In our everyday lives, we tell stories and invite other people to do so by asking questions such as "What happened at work today?" and "What did you do last weekend?" We are disappointed when the answer is "Nothing much." We may be equally disappointed when a person doesn't give us enough details or gives us too many and spoils the effect. After all, we are interested in people's stories and in the people who tell them. We like narratives.

What is a narrative? A narrative is an account of an incident or a series of incidents that make up a complete and significant action. A narrative can be as short as a joke, as long as a novel, or anything between, including a single paragraph. Each narrative has five properties.

Situation

Situation is the background for the action. The situation may be described only briefly, or it may even be implied. ("To celebrate my seventeenth birthday, I went to the Department of Motor Vehicles to take my practical test for my driver's license.")

Conflict

Conflict is friction, such as a problem in the surroundings, with another person(s), or within the individual. The conflict, which is at the heart of each story, produces struggle. ("It was raining and my appointment was the last one of the day. The examiner was a serious, weary-looking man who reminded me of a bad boss I once had, and I was nervous.")

Struggle

Struggle, which need not be physical, is the manner of dealing with the conflict. The struggle adds action or engagement and generates the plot. ("After grinding on the ignition because the engine was already on, I had trouble finding the windshield wiper control. Next I forgot to signal until after I had pulled away from the curb. As we crept slowly down the rain-glazed street, the examiner told me to take the emergency brake off. All the while I listened to his pen scratching on his clipboard. 'Pull over and park,' he said solemnly.")

Outcome

Outcome is the result of the struggle. ("After I parked the car, the examiner told me to relax, and then he talked to me about school. When we continued, somehow I didn't make any errors, and I got my license.")

Meaning

Meaning is the significance of the story, which may be deeply philosophical or simple, stated or implied ("calmness promotes calmness").

These components are present in some way in all the many forms of the narrative. They are enhanced by the use of various devices like the following:

- *Description* (the use of specific details to advance action, with images to make readers see, smell, taste, hear, and feel)

  "the *rain-glazed street*"

  "listened to his *pen scratching*"

- *Dialogue* (the exact words of the speakers, enclosed in quotation marks)

  "*Pull over and park,*" he said solemnly.

- *Transitional words* (words, such as *after, finally, following, later, next, soon,* and *when,* that move a story forward, for narratives are usually presented in chronological order)

  "*Next* I forgot to"

  "*After* I parked the car"

Most narratives written as college assignments have an expository purpose (that is, they explain a specified idea). Often the narrative will be merely an extended example. Therefore, the meaning of the narrative is exceedingly important and should be clear, whether it is stated or implied.

Examining Narrative Paragraphs

Student Writer

The Customer Is Always Right

Jack Mullens

When the manager of a business must choose between being fair to an employee or risking bad public relations, the employee may have to lose face—and a considerable portion of his or her paycheck.

Topic sentence   "The customer is always right" is a saying that took on new meaning for me soon after I acquired my first job, as attendant in a gas station. It was a Union station, and the manager regularly reminded us workers

Situation   that we were "Minutemen" and that cheerful, fast service was our reputation. After all, he was bucking the trend toward completely self-service stations. I soon developed a routine for quick service—insert nozzle, start gas, check oil, clean windshield, stop gas, remove nozzle, collect money, or process credit card. At times the unexpected would occur and upset my routine. The "unexpected" on this occasion was a co-worker telling me he couldn't work the next day, and I would have to work a double shift. The result was

Conflict   that <u>I skipped one part of my routine</u>: the

Struggle   <u>of metal against metal</u>, the <u>snap of the hose</u>, and the <u>gushing of gas</u>. Immediately the manager appeared and <u>shut off the main gas valve</u>. Then the customer was out of his car, pointing to <u>a shallow, two-inch scratch in his paint job</u>—a faded paint job that already had several much larger scratches. The manager apologized, said I was new, and promised "we" would pay when the customer brought in an estimate. After the customer left, the manager explained that *I* would pay out of my wages, and I certainly didn't object. But a few days later, the customer returned with an estimate for three hundred and forty-two dollars. The manager didn't blink as he wrote out a check. After the man left, the manager said to me, "It's public

Outcome   relations. I couldn't argue with him." <u>I worked for more than a month to pay for the</u>

Meaning and Concluding sentence   <u>scratch.</u> "<u>The customer is always right</u>" <u>may be a necessary slogan, but at times the customer may be partly wrong.</u>

PROFESSIONAL WRITER

Voice Like Twigs Underfoot

Maxine Hong Kingston

Now a celebrated writer, Maxine Hong Kingston was once so deficient in English speech that she flunked kindergarten. In this passage taken from her book The Woman Warrior: Memoirs of a Childhood Among Ghosts *(1976), she tells about one of her early experiences as a frightened girl caught between two cultures.*

1   Not all of the children who were silent at American school found voice at Chinese school. One new teacher said each of us had to get up and recite in front of the class, who was to listen. My sister and I had memorized the lesson perfectly. We said it to each other at home, one chanting, one listening. The teacher called on my sister to recite first. It was the first time a teacher had called on the second-born to go first. My sister was scared. She glanced at me and looked away; I looked down at my desk. I hoped that she could do it because if she could, then I would have to. She opened her mouth and a voice came out that wasn't a whisper, but it wasn't a proper voice either. I hoped that she would not cry, fear breaking up her voice like twigs underfoot. She sounded as if she were trying to sing through weeping and strangling. She did not pause to stop to end the embarrassment. She kept going until she said the last word, and then she sat down. When it was my turn, the same voice came out, a crippled animal running on broken legs. You could hear splinters in my voice, bones rubbing jagged against one another. I was loud, though. I was glad I didn't whisper.

█ EXERCISE 1

In your own words, identify the parts of Kingston's narrative.

Situation: _____

_____

Conflict: _____

_____

Struggle: _____

_____

Outcome: _____

_____

Meaning: _____

_____

PRACTICING NARRATIVE PATTERNS

▌ EXERCISE 2

Fill in the blanks to complete each narrative pattern.

1. Lost and Found

   (situation)   I. Person taking store money deposit bag to bank

   (conflict)   II. Person loses bag

   (struggle)   III. _____

   (outcome)   IV. _____

   (meaning)   V. _____

2. Good Samaritan

   (situation)   I. Driver with flat tire, dead of night

   (conflict)   II. No spare tire

   (struggle)   III. _____

   (outcome)   IV. _____

   (meaning)   V. _____

TOPICS FOR NARRATIVE PARAGRAPHS

Reading-Related Topics

1. "The Customer Is Always Right": Write a narrative paragraph in which you discuss how you had to lose face in order to achieve a personal, company, or group goal in a work, school, sports, or family situation.
2. "Voice Like Twigs Underfoot": Write a narrative paragraph about something you had to struggle to do, like make a presentation or talk to someone you admired, held in high esteem, or were afraid of.

Career-Related Topics

3. Write a narrative paragraph about a work-related encounter between a manager and a worker, and briefly explain the significance of the event.
4. Write a narrative paragraph about an encounter between a customer and a salesperson. Explain what went right and wrong.
5. Write a narrative paragraph about how a person solved a work-related problem.
6. Write a narrative paragraph about a salesperson's dealing with a customer's complaint. Critique the procedure.

General Topics

7. Write a narrative paragraph about a personal experience that you might characterize as the most amusing, sad, terrifying, satisfying, stupid, rewarding, self-centered, generous, stingy, loving, thoughtful, cruel, regrettable, educational, corrupting, sinful, virtuous, or disgusting thing you have done or witnessed. Keep in mind that you are writing about a single event or a portion of that event.
8. Write a narrative paragraph about the first time you did something, such as the first time you dated, kissed romantically, spoke formally in public, entered a new school, worked for pay, drove an automobile, rode a bicycle or motorcycle, danced, received a traffic citation, met a celebrity, or played a game.

WRITER'S GUIDELINES AT A GLANCE: NARRATION

1. Use this checklist to be sure you have a complete narrative.

   ☐ Situation (at beginning)
   ☐ Conflict
   ☐ Struggle
   ☐ Outcome
   ☐ Meaning

2. Use these devices as appropriate:

   ▪ Images (sight, sound, smell, taste, touch) and other details to advance action
   ▪ Dialogue
   ▪ Transitional words (such as *after, finally, following, later, next, soon, when*) to enhance chronological order

4

Description: Moving Through Space and Time

WRITING DESCRIPTIVE PARAGRAPHS

Description is the use of words to represent the appearance or nature of something. Often called a word picture, description attempts to present its subject for the mind's eye. In doing so, it does not merely become an indifferent camera; instead, it selects details that will depict something well. Just what details the descriptive writer selects will depend on several factors, especially the type of description and the dominant impression in the passage.

Types of Description

On the basis of treatment of subject material, description is customarily divided into two types: objective and subjective.

Effective objective description presents the subject clearly and directly as it exists outside the realm of feelings. If you are explaining the function of the heart, the characteristics of a computer chip, or the renovation of a manufacturing facility, your description would probably feature specific, impersonal details. Most technical and scientific writing is objective in that sense. It is likely to be practical and utilitarian, making little use of speculation and poetic technique while focusing on details of sight.

Effective subjective description is also concerned with clarity and it may be direct, but it conveys a feeling about the subject and sets a mood while making a point. Because most expression involves personal views, even when it explains by analysis, subjective description (often called "emotional description") has a broader range of uses than objective description.

39

Descriptive passages can have a combination of objective and subjective description; only the larger context of the passage will reveal the main intent.

Imagery

In order to convey your main concern effectively to readers, you will have to give some sensory impressions. These sensory impressions, collectively called *imagery*, refer to that which can be experienced by the senses—what we can see, smell, taste, hear, and touch.

Subjective description is more likely to use images and words rich in associations than does objective description. But just as a fine line cannot always be drawn between the objective and the subjective, a fine line cannot always be drawn between word choice in one and in the other. However, we can say with certainty that whatever the type of description, careful word choice will always be important. Consider these points about precise diction:

General and Specific Words/Abstract and Concrete Words

To move from the general to the specific is to move from the whole class or body to the individual(s); for example:

General	Specific	More Specific
food	hamburger	Hefty Burger
mess	grease	oil slicks on table
drink	soda	mug of root beer
odor	smell from grill	smell of frying onions

Words are classified as abstract or concrete depending on what they refer to. *Abstract words* refer to qualities or ideas: *good, ordinary, ultimate, truth, beauty, maturity, love. Concrete words* refer to substances or things; they have reality: *onions, grease, buns, tables, food.* The specific concrete words, sometimes called *concrete particulars*, often support generalizations effectively and convince the reader of the accuracy of the account.

Dominant Impression

Never try to give all of the details in description; instead, be selective, picking only those that you need to make a dominant impression, always taking into account the knowledge and attitudes of your readers. Remember, description is not photographic. If you wish to describe a person, select only those traits that will project your dominant impression. If you wish to describe a landscape, do not give all the details that you might find in a picture; just pick the details that support what you want to say. That extremely important dominant impression is directly linked to your purpose and is created by choosing and arranging images, figurative language, and revealing details.

Order: Time and Space

All of these details must have some order. Time and space are the main controlling factors in most description.

If you were describing something that was not changing, such as a room, you would be concerned with space and give directions to the reader such as

> *next to, below, under, above, behind, in front of, beyond, in the foreground, in the background, to the left, to the right.*

If you were describing something that was changing, such as a butterfly going through metamorphosis, you would be concerned mainly with time and use transitional words such as

> *first, second, then, soon, finally, while, after, next, later, now, before.*

If you were walking through an area—so that the setting was changing—you would use both time and space for order.

Useful Procedure for Writing Description

What is your subject? (school campus during summer vacation)
What is the dominant impression? (deserted)
What is the situation? (You are walking across the campus in early August.)
What is the order of details? (time and place)
What details support the dominant impression?

1. (smell of flowers and cut grass rather than food and smoke and perfume)
2. (dust accumulated on white porcelain drinking fountain)
3. (sound of the wind, wildlife, and silence rather than people)
4. (crunch of dead leaves underfoot)
5. (echo of footsteps)

EXAMINING DESCRIPTIVE PARAGRAPHS
Student Writer

Latchkey

Janice Hill

Janice Hill had no trouble identifying the possession she most de-spised. It was a key she carried around her neck, first on a thong, then on a chain. It seemed to take on a life of its own as it hung there. She probably would have preferred a millstone or even an albatross.

Topic sentence

The thing I hated most when I was growing up was a metal object about two inches long. The top part was of an oval shape turned on the side, with a hole at the top middle. Down from the oval was a flat shaft, which was

Sight images

straight on one side, notched irregularly on the other, grooved in a straight line near the middle on each flat side, and pointed at the end. At the top, near the middle of the inch-long oval was the word *Master.* Oddly that's what it was to me—my master. It was my latchkey. When I went to school, it went everywhere I did. One day I took it off at school and misplaced it. My mother was very angry. I said I hated the leather thong from

Smell

which it hung because it was ugly and smelled of sweat. She replaced that with a silver chain, and said I should never take the key off. Each day I would wear that chain and key, always inside my sweater, shirt, or

Touch   blouse. In the winter it was <u>icicle cold</u> as it dangled against my skinny chest. In the summer it was <u>hot</u> against my sweaty skin, sticking like a clammy leech. Because I was forbidden to take it off by myself, even upon coming home, I always bent forward when I inserted it into the lock, my sad, sometimes

Sight   scared, <u>face reflecting with weird distortions</u> in the brass door knob. I

Sound   inserted the key, turned it with a <u>click,</u> and removed it. After three years of my life with the detested key, I had to bend way over to turn it in the lock, my head pressed against the solid wood door. By that time the key and

Sight   the chain had worn <u>smooth</u> in places, and the <u>crisscross pattern</u> around the name had <u>darkened.</u> I always feared what lurked inside that house. Though I had a neighbor I could call if I needed help, that key always

Concluding sentence   represented loneliness and fear. <u>I was glad when my mother got a new job with shorter hours, and I was no longer a latchkey kid</u>.

PROFESSIONAL WRITER

The Road to Cedar City

William Least Heat-Moon

William Trogdon, of English-Irish-Osage ancestry, writes under the pen name William Least Heat-Moon. Traveling around the country in an old van he named Ghost Dancing, he sought out interesting locales on secondary highways marked in blue on road

maps. His descriptive narratives of these adventures were published in the best-selling book Blue Highways *(1982), from which this paragraph is taken.*

At dusk I considered going into the Coral Sand Dunes for the night, but I'd had enough warmth and desert for a while, so I pushed north toward Cedar Breaks in the severe and beautiful Markagunt Plateau. The cool would refresh me. Sporadic splats of rain, not enough to pay attention to, hit the windshield. I turned onto Utah 14, the cross-mountain road to Cedar City. In the dim light of a mountainous sky, I could just make out a large sign:

ELEVATION 10,000 FEET
ROAD MAY BE IMPASSIBLE
DURING WINTER MONTHS.

So? It was nearly May. The rain popped, then stopped, popped and stopped. The incline became steeper and light rain fell steadily, rolling red desert dust off the roof; I hadn't hit showers since east Texas. It was good. The pleasant cool turned to cold, and I switched on the heater. The headlights glared off snowbanks edging closer to the highway as it climbed, and the rain became sleet. That's when I began thinking I might have made a little miscalculation. I looked for a place to turn around, but there was only narrow, twisted road. The sleet got heavier, and the headlights were cutting only thirty feet into it. Maybe I could drive above and out of the storm. At eight thousand feet, the wind came up—a rough, nasty wind that bullied me about the slick road. Lear,* daring the storm to "strike flat the thick rotundity of the world," cries, "Blow, winds! . . . Rage! Blow!" And that's just what they did.

▌ EXERCISE 1

1. What is the dominant impression of the paragraph by William Least Heat-Moon? _____

_____

_____

_____

*Lear: The main character in William Shakespeare's play King Lear.

_____

_____

2.Give an example of three of the senses (sight, sound, taste, touch,
smell) used in this description. _____

_____

_____

_____

_____

_____

3. Is the description organized by time or space or both? _____

_____

_____

_____

_____

_____

PRACTICING DESCRIPTIVE PATTERNS

EXERCISE 2

Fill in the blanks to complete the following description.

A Produce Area in a Supermarket
(Dominant impression: Diversity)

  I. Food displays (sight—color, shape)

    A. _____

    B. _____

    C. _____

  II. Smells (from vegetables, fruits)

    A. _____

    B. _____

III. Textures (smooth or rough to touch)

    A. _____

    B. _____

IV. Taste (samples of sweet/sour, ripe/unripe)

    A. _____

    B. _____

TOPICS FOR DESCRIPTIVE PARAGRAPHS

Reading-Related Topics

1. "Latchkey": Use this paragraph as a model to write a descriptive paragraph about something you prized or despised, such as a gift from a grandparent, braces for your teeth, a cast for a broken bone, a piece of sports equipment, or an article of clothing.
2. "The Road to Cedar City": Write about a dramatic part of a difficult trip you (as driver or passenger) took under bad conditions, such as fog, snow, rain, windstorm, hail, heat, or traffic congestion. Be very specific in stating the place; consider quoting from a road sign as Heat-Moon did. Use both time and space to give order to your descriptive paragraph.

Career-Related Topics

3. Describe a well-furnished, well-functioning office or other work area. Be specific.
4. Describe a product, with special attention to the dominant trait that gives the product its reputation.
5. Describe a specific person properly groomed and attired for a particular job or interview. Be specific in giving details pertaining to the person and in naming the place and/or situation. If you like, objectively describe yourself as that specific person.

General Topics

Objective Description

Give your topic some kind of frame. As you develop your purpose, consider the knowledge and attitudes of your readers. You might be describing a lung for a biology instructor, a geode for a geology instructor, a painting for an art instructor, or a comet for an astronomy instructor. Or maybe you could pose as the seller of an object such as a desk, a table, or a bicycle. Try some of the following topics:

6. A simple object, such as pencil, a pair of scissors, a cup, a sock, a dollar bill, a coin, a ring, a notebook.
7. A human organ, such as a heart, a liver, a lung, or a kidney.
8. A visible part of your body, such as a toe, a finger, an ear, a nose, an eye.
9. A construction, such as a room, a desk, a chair, a table.
10. A mechanism, such as a bicycle, a tricycle, a wagon, a car, a motorcycle, a can opener, a stapler.

Subjective Description

The following topics should also be presented in the context of a purpose other than just writing a description. Your intent can be as simple as giving a subjective reaction to your subject. But unless you are dealing with one of those topics that you can present reflectively or a topic interesting in itself, you will usually need some kind of situation. The narrative frame (something happening) is especially useful in providing order and vitality to writing. Here are two possibilities for you to consider:

11. Personalize a trip to a supermarket, a stadium, an airport, an unusual house, a mall, a beach, a court, a place of worship, a club, a business, a library, or a police station. Deal with a simple conflict in one of those places, while emphasizing descriptive details.
12. Pick a high point in any event, and describe a few seconds of it. Think about how a scene can be captured by a video camera, and then give focus by applying the dominant impression principle, using the images of sight, sound, taste, touch, and smell that are relevant. The event might be a ball game, a graduation ceremony, a wedding ceremony, a funeral, a dance, a concert, a family gathering, a class meeting, a rally, a riot, a robbery, a fight, a proposal, or a meal. Focus on a body of subject material that you can cover effectively in the paragraph you write.

WRITER'S GUIDELINES AT A GLANCE: DESCRIPTION

1. In an objective description, use direct, practical language and usually appeal mainly to the sense of sight.
2. In an emotional description, appeal to the reader's feelings, especially through the use of figurative language and images of sight, sound, smell, taste, and touch.

3. Use specific and concrete words if appropriate.
4. Be sure that readers can answer the following questions:

> What is the subject of this description?
> What is the dominant impression?
> What is the situation?
> What is the order of details—time, space, or both?
> What details support the dominant impression?

5

Exemplification: Writing with Examples

WRITING PARAGRAPHS OF EXEMPLIFICATION

Exemplification means using examples to explain, convince, or amuse. Lending interest and information to writing, exemplification is one of the most common and effective ways of developing ideas. Examples may be developed in a sentence or more, or they may be only phrases or even single words, as in the following sentence: "Children like packaged breakfast foods, such as *Wheaties, Cheerios,* and *Rice Krispies.*"

Characteristics of Good Examples

As supporting information, the best examples are vivid, specific, and representative. These three qualities are closely linked, and collectively, they must support the topic sentence. The *vivid* example attracts attention. Then through a memorable presentation and the use of identifying names, the example becomes *specific* to the reader. A good example must also be *representative;* that is, it must be experienced as typical, so that it can be the basis for a generalization.

Finally, and most important, the connection between the example and the topic sentence must be clear. A bizarre case of cheating may be fascinating in itself (vivid and specific), but in a paragraph on "the hard work of cheating," it must also support the topic sentence. The reader should say, in effect, "That's interesting, convincing, and memorable. Though it's unusual, I can see that it's typical of what goes on."

49

Techniques for Finding Examples

Writing a good paragraph of exemplification begins, as always, with prewriting. The techniques you use will depend on what you are writing about. Assuming that you begin with a topic idea, one useful technique is listing. Base your list on what you have read, heard, and experienced. Here is a list on the broad topic "cheating at school":

> When I copied homework
> Looking at a friend's test answers
> A student with hand signals
> Jake and his electronic system
> Time for planned cheating
> Those who got caught
> A person who bought a research paper
> Jess, who copied from me
> The Internet "Cheaters" source
> The two students who exchanged identities
> More work than it's worth
> More stress than it's worth

Connecting Examples with Purpose

Here is the final paragraph on the topic "the hard work of cheating."

> Cheating students often put themselves under more stress than honest students. I remember someone in my junior composition class who needed a research paper, so he found a source and bought one for seventy-five dollars. The first trouble was that he had to submit the work in stages: the topic, the working bibliography, the note cards, the outline, the rough draft, and the final. Therefore, he went to the library and started working backwards. Of course, he couldn't turn in only the bib cards actually used in the paper, and next he had to make out note

cards for the material he "would be" documenting, and even make out more. After having all kinds of trouble, he realized that the bought paper was of "A" quality, whereas he had been a "C" student. He went back to his source and was told he should change the sentence structure and so on to make the paper weaker. Finally he dropped the class after spending more time on his paper than I **Concluding** did on mine. He also suffered more anxiety **sentence** than the students who put in the most work on their papers.

EXAMINING PARAGRAPHS OF EXEMPLIFICATION

Student Writer

The Fighting Founding Mothers

Maxine Johnson

Some people are surprised to discover that among the soldiers who fought gallantly in the War of Independence were numerous women. Mary Hayes, who once had a cannonball sail between her knees and tear her dress, actually received a veteran's pension. U.S. history student Maxine Johnson provides some good examples here to support her topic sentence.

Topic People argue a lot about the prospects of **sentence** women in the military fighting in combat, but in the War of Independence, several women distinguished themselves in combat situations. In 1775, Paul Revere got the main credit for riding to warn the Patriots that the British were coming in a military move on Concord and Lexington, Massachusetts. The fact is that although he did warn some

Patriots, he was stopped by the British. Who

did get through? Several people, including

Example Sybil Ludington, a teenage woman who

fearlessly rode her horse like the wind.

Another famous woman was known as Molly

Example Pitcher. Her real name was <u>Mary Hayes</u>. She

went with her husband to the battlefield,

where she brought the men pitchers of water

(hence her nickname) and helped load the

cannon her husband fired. When her husband

was shot at the Battle of Monmouth in 1778,

she took over the cannon and fought bravely.

At the end of the battle, won by the

Patriots, she carried a wounded man for two

Concluding miles. <u>More than two hundred years ago, these</u>
sentence

<u>women proved that their gender can be</u>

<u>soldiers in every sense.</u>

PROFESSIONAL WRITER

Everything for a Price

Pierre Berton

Taken from The Klondike Fever: The Life and Death of the Last
Great Gold Rush, *this paragraph shows that in the frontier town of
Dawson, Yukon Territory, Canada, in 1898, almost everything was
available—for a price. Born in Dawson, Pierre Berton is a television
commentator, a journalist, and the author of four other books.*

1   You could buy almost anything under the sun during that
climactic summer in Dawson City. You could buy clothes and
furs, moccasins and plug hats, shoes and jewelry, fresh grapes,
opera glasses, safety pins, and ice cream. You could buy peanuts
and pink lemonade, patent-leather shoes, yellow-jacketed

novels, cribbage boards, ostrich feathers, and oxen on the hoof. You could, if you were so inclined, buy for one hundred dollars the tusk of a prehistoric mammoth, dredged out of the frozen ground by prospectors—or, for twenty-five cents, a slicker coat with a bad cigar thrown in as premium. You could have your palm read, your picture taken, your back massaged, or your teeth filled with nuggets. You could buy Bibles and sets of Shakespeare and pairs of gold-scales by the hundreds, for these had been standard equipment with almost every man. You could buy rifles by the gross at one dollar each; they were worthless in a town where nobody was allowed to pack a gun. Many men stripped off the barrels to use as pipes for transmitting steam into the frozen ground and thawing the soil at the mines, and others bought them by the score and shipped them back Outside at a profit.

EXERCISE 1

1. Underline the topic sentence of "Everything for a Price."

2. Berton uses many examples.What is the effect of his piling example upon example?

3. What aspects of life in frontier Dawson are implied by Berton's selection of examples?

4. What do the examples tell you about the people in Dawson in 1898?

PRACTICING PATTERNS OF EXEMPLIFICATION

EXERCISE 2

Fill in the blanks to add more examples that support the topic sentence.

1. Topic sentence: Just walking through my favorite mall (or shopping center) shows me that the world is smaller than it used to be.

   I. People of different cultures (with specific examples)

   II. Foods of different cultures (with specific examples)

III. _____

IV. _____

2. Topic sentence: Driving to work (or school) this month and observing the behavior of other drivers have convinced me that road rage has invaded my community.

    I. A man honking his horn impatiently at an elderly driver

   II. _____

   III. _____

TOPICS FOR PARAGRAPHS OF EXEMPLIFICATION

Reading-Related Topics

1. "The Fighting Founding Mothers": Use an example or examples to write a paragraph about the involvement of Native Americans or African Americans in the War of Independence (or about any underrepresented or misrepresented group in any war or movement).
2. Use an example or examples to write about men found in unexpected roles, places, or activities.
3. "Everything for a Price": Using the Berton paragraph as a model, write a paragraph about the different kinds of majors offered at your college and the courses that support such majors. You might concentrate on unusual majors and rather highly specialized or unusual courses. Be specific. Your topic sentence might be "A student can major in almost anything at _____." Then develop your topic sentence with specific examples.
4. Using the Berton paragraph as a model, write about an antiques store, a garage sale, a thrift store, or a used auto parts store, stressing the idea that almost anything can be bought there.

Career-Related Topics

Use specific examples to support one of the following statements as applied to business or work:

5. It's not what you know; it's who you know.
6. Don't burn your bridges.
7. Like Lego, business is a matter of connections.
8. Tact is the lubricant that oils the wheels of industry.

9. The customer is always right.
10. Money is honey, my little sonny, and the rich man's joke is always funny.
11. If you take care of the pennies, the dollars will take care of themselves.
12. A kind word turns away wrath.

General Topics

Make a judgmental statement about a social issue you believe in strongly and then use an example or examples to illustrate your point. These are some possible topics:

13. The price of groceries is too high.
14. Professional athletes are paid too much.
15. A person buying a new car may get a lemon.
16. Drivers sometimes openly ignore the laws on a selective basis.
17. Politicians should be watched.
18. Working and going to school is tough.
19. Working, parenting, and going to school is tough.

WRITER'S GUIDELINES AT A GLANCE: EXEMPLIFICATION

1. Use examples to explain, convince, or amuse.
2. Use examples that are vivid, specific, and representative.

   - Vivid examples attract attention.
   - Specific examples are identifiable.
   - Representative examples are typical and therefore the basis for generalizations.

3. Tie your examples clearly to your topic sentence.
4. Draw your examples from what you have read, heard, and experienced.
5. Brainstorm a list of possible examples before you write.

6

Analysis by Division: Examining the Parts

Writing Paragraphs of Analysis by Division

If you need to explain how something works or exists as a unit, you will write an analysis by division. You will break down a unit (your subject) into its parts and explain how each part functions in relation to the operation or existence of the whole. The most important word here is *unit*. You begin with something that can stand alone or can be regarded separately, such as a poem, a heart, a painting, a car, a bike, a person, a school, or a committee.

The following procedure will guide you in writing an analysis by division. Move from subject to principle, to division, to relationship:

Step 1: Begin with something that is a unit.
Step 2: State one principle by which the unit can function.
Step 3: Divide the unit into parts according to that principle.
Step 4: Discuss each of the parts in relation to the unit.

Here's how this general procedure is applied to a real object (unit).

Step 1: For the unit, we choose a pencil.
Step 2: For our principle (the purpose or role), we see the pencil as a writing instrument.
Step 3: For dividing the unit into parts based on the principle of a pencil as a writing instrument, we divide the pencil into an eraser, an eraser holder, a wooden barrel, and a thin graphite core with a sharpened point.
Step 4: Here is our discussion of the parts in relation to the unit. "At the top of the wooden barrel is a strip of metal

56

encircling an eraser and clamping it to the barrel. In the center of the barrel is a core of graphite that can be sharpened to a point at the end and used for writing. The eraser is used to remove marks made by the graphite point. Thus we have a complete writing tool, one that marks and erases marks."

Like many things, a pencil can be regarded in different ways. For example, an artist might not consider a pencil mainly as a writing tool. Instead, an artist might look at a pencil and see it as an object that could be used as a subject in a still-life painting. Here is how an artist might follow the procedure:

Step 1: For the unit, I choose a pencil.

Step 2: For the principle or way of regarding the unit, I see the pencil as an object of simple functional beauty.

Step 3: For the division into parts based on my principle, I divide the pencil into texture, shape, and color.

Step 4: For the discussion of parts in relation to the unit, I explain how the textures of the metal, graphite, and wood, along with their shapes and colors, produce a beautiful object.

Either treatment of the same unit, the pencil, is valid. But mixing the treatments by applying more than one principle at a time causes problems. For example, if we were to say that a pencil has an eraser, an eraser holder, a wooden barrel, a graphite core, and a beautiful coat of yellow paint, we would have an illogical analysis by division, because all parts but the "beautiful coat of yellow paint" relate to the pencil as a writing instrument.

Organization

In a paragraph of analysis by division, the main parts are likely to be the main points of your outline or main extensions of your cluster. If they are anything else, reconsider your organization. For the pencil, your outline might look like this:

I. Eraser
II. Eraser holder
III. Wooden barrel
IV. Graphite core with point at one end

Sequence of Parts

The order in which you discuss the parts will vary according to the nature of the unit and the way in which you view it. Here are some possible sequences for organizing the parts of a unit.

> *Time:* The sequence of the parts in your paragraph can be based on time (if you are dealing with something that functions on its own, such as a heart, with the parts presented in relation to stages of the function).
>
> *Space:* If your unit is a visual object, especially if, like the pencil, it does nothing by itself, you may discuss the parts in relation to space. In the example above, the parts of the pencil begin at the top with the eraser and end at the bottom with the pencil point.
>
> *Emphasis:* Since the most emphatic part of any piece of writing is the end (the second most emphatic point is the beginning), consider placing the most significant part of the unit at the end. In the example, both space and emphasis govern the placement of the pencil point at the end of the order.

EXAMINING PARAGRAPHS OF ANALYSIS BY DIVISION

Student Writer

More Than Ordinary

Nancy Samuels

Faced with writing on the topic of "an example of a hero, with a discussion of the hero's traits [analysis by division]," Nancy Samuels didn't have to go to the library. Right in her household she found her subject—her mother. She writes about an ordinary person who faced a difficult challenge and succeeded in a situation in which others gave up.

Topic sentence	<u>My mother is the best example of a hero I can think of</u>. No one will read about her in a book about heroes, but in her small circle of friends, no one doubts her heroism. Certainly

my younger brother doesn't. He is the special
beneficiary of her heroism. He was in an
accident when he was five years old, and the
doctor told us that he would never walk again.
My mother listened respectfully, but she

Trait   didn't believe him. She had <u>optimism.</u> She went
to another doctor and then another. Finally
she found one who prescribed exercises. She
worked with my brother for three years. Day

Trait   after dismal day, she <u>persevered.</u> It wasn't
just her working with him that helped my
brother. It was her raw courage in the face of
failure. My brother worked with her. They both

Trait   were <u>courageous.</u> We other family members
weren't. To us my brother and mother were
acting like a couple of blind fools. We
thought my mother especially, the leader, was
in prolonged denial. But in three years my
brother was walking. He won't be an athlete;
nevertheless, he gets around. We're proud of
him, but we know—and he knows—that without
Mother he would never have walked. Of course,
she's not a miracle worker. Most of the time,
doctors are right, and some injured people can
never walk. But the ones like my brother, who
somewhere have that hidden ability, need that
special someone like my mother. She's more

Concluding
sentence   than ordinary. <u>She's a hero</u>.

PROFESSIONAL WRITER

The Zones of the Sea

Leonard Engel et al.

In this paragraph reprinted from The Sea, *published by Time-Life Books, the authors show that the sea can be divided into four zones.*

1   The life of the ocean is divided into distinct realms, each with its own group of creatures that feed upon each other and depend on each other in different ways. There is, first of all, the tidal zone, where land and sea meet. Then comes the realm of the shallow seas around the continents, which goes down to about 500 feet. It is in these two zones that the vast majority of marine life occurs. The deep ocean adds two regions, the zone of light and the zone of perpetual darkness. In the clear waters of the western Pacific, light could still be seen at a depth of 1,000 feet through the portholes of the *Trieste* on its seven-mile dive. But for practical purposes the zone of light ends at about 600 feet. Below that level there is too little light to support the growth of the "grass" of the sea—the tiny, single-celled green plants whose ability to form sugar and starch with the aid of sunlight makes them the base of the great food pyramid of the ocean.

EXERCISE 1

1. What are the four zones of the sea?

2. Is the paragraph organized by space or by time?

3. What characterizes each zone?

4. Draw a simple cross section of the sea to show the four zones. Make it as elaborate as you like.

PRACTICING PATTERNS OF ANALYSIS BY DIVISION

EXERCISE 2

Fill in the blanks to complete each analysis by division.

1. Unit: Federal government

   Principle: Division of power

   Parts based on the principle:

   I. Executive

   II. _____

   III. _____

2. Unit: Good boss

   Principle: Effectiveness in leading a work force

   Parts based on the principle:

   I. Fair

   II. _____

   III. _____

   IV. _____

TOPICS FOR PARAGRAPHS OF ANALYSIS BY DIVISION

Reading-Related Topics

1. "More Than Ordinary": Write about an ordinary person who has struggled mightily and deserves the title *hero.* Structure your piece around the person's achievements and traits, especially the traits.
2. Write a paragraph of analysis by division about a person who is an excellent role model for you or others you know.
3. "The Zones of the Sea": Using this paragraph as a model, write about the layers of something else, such as skin, bone, a tree, the atmosphere, the earth, or a snow field. Consult an encyclopedia or textbook for specific information on your topic or for terminology, but be sure to use your own sentences to write the paragraph.

Career-Related Topics

4. Explain how the parts of a particular product function together as a unit.
5. Explain how each of several qualities of a specific person, such as his or her intelligence, sincerity, knowledgeability, ability to

communicate, manner, attitude, and appearance, makes that individual an effective salesperson, manager, or employee.

6. Explain how the demands or requirements for a particular job represent a comprehensive picture of that job.

General Topics

7. In a paragraph of analysis by division, discuss the qualities that make someone or something successful or praiseworthy. Select one of these subjects:

> A specific performer (a singer, a dancer, an actor, or a musician)
> A team, a company, a school, a class, an organization
> A movie, a television program, a music video, a video game
> A family, a marriage, a relationship, a club

Begin with a topic sentence such as this (modify it later if you find it too mechanical): "_____'s success can be attributed to three (or four) qualities." The qualities would, of course, become the main parts of your outline.

8. Discuss how a physical object works, perhaps a part of the body (heart, ear, lungs); a part of a car (carburetor, water pump); or an object like a tape player, a stapler, a pencil sharpener, or a hair dryer.

WRITER'S GUIDELINES AT A GLANCE: ANALYSIS BY DIVISION

1. Follow the procedure discussed in this chapter from (1) unit to (2) principle to (3) parts to (4) discussion.
2. Write a strong topic sentence to unify your writing.
3. Present the parts in a way that promotes order. Consider time, space, and emphasis.
4. Emphasize how the parts function in relation to the operation of the whole unit.
5. Your basic outline will probably look like this:
   I. Part 1
   II. Part 2
   III. Part 3

7

Process Analysis: Writing About Doing

WRITING PARAGRAPHS OF PROCESS ANALYSIS

If you have any doubt about how freqeuntly we use process analysis, just think about how many times you have heard people say, "How do you do it?" or "How is [was] it done?" Even when you are not hearing those questions, you are posing them yourself when you need to make something, cook a meal, assemble an item, take some medicine, repair something, or figure out what happened. In your college classes, you may have to discover how osmosis occurs, how a rock changes form, how a mountain was formed, how a battle was won, or how a bill goes through the legislature.

If you need to explain how to do something or how something was (is) done, you will write a paper of *process analysis*. You will break down your topic into stages, explaining each so that your reader can duplicate or understand the process.

Two Types of Process Analysis: Directive and Informative

The questions How do I do it? and How is (was) it done? will lead you into two different types of process analysis—directive and informative.

Directive process analysis explains how to do something. As the name suggests, it gives directions and tells the reader how to do something. It says, for example, "Read me, and you can bake a pie (tune up your car, read a book, write an essay, take some medicine)." Because it is presented directly to the reader, it usually addresses the reader as "you," or it implies the "you" by saying something such as "First [you] purchase a large, fat wombat, and then

63

[you] . . ." In the same way, this textbook addresses you or implies "you" because it is a long how-to-do-it (directive process analysis) statement.

Informative process analysis explains how something was (is) done by giving data (information). Whereas the directive process analysis tells you what to do in the future, the informative process analysis tells you what has occurred or what is occurring. If it is something in nature, such as the formation of a mountain, you can read and understand the process by which it emerged. In this type of process analysis, you do not tell the reader what to do; therefore, you do not use the words *you* or *your.*

WORKING WITH STAGES

Preparation   In the first stage of the directive type of process analysis, list the materials or equipment needed for the process and discuss the necessary setup arrangements. For some topics, this stage will also provide technical terms and definitions. The degree to which this stage is detailed will depend on both the subject itself and the expected knowledge and experience of the projected audience.

The informative type of process analysis may begin with background or context rather than with preparation. For example, a statement explaining how mountains form might begin with a description of a flat portion of the earth made up of plates that are arranged like a jigsaw puzzle.

Steps   The actual process will be presented here. Each step must be explained clearly and directly, and phrased to accommodate the audience. The language, especially in directive process analysis, is likely to be simple and concise; however, avoid dropping words such as *and, a, an, the,* and *of,* and thereby lapsing into "recipe language." The steps may be accompanied by explanations about why certain procedures are necessary and how not following directions carefully can lead to trouble.

Order   The order will usually be chronological (time based) in some sense. Certain transitional words are commonly used to promote coherence: *first, second, third, then, soon, now, next, finally, at last, therefore, consequently,* and—especially for informative process analysis—words used to show the passage of time such as hours, days of the week, and so on.

Basic Forms

- Consider using this form for the directive process (with topics such as how to cook something or how to fix something).
  - I. Preparation
    - A.
    - B.
    - C.
  - II. Steps
    - A.
    - B.
    - C.
    - D.
- Consider using this form for the informative process (with topics such as how a volcano functions or how a battle was won).
  - I. Background or context
    - A.
    - B.
    - C.
  - II. Change or development (narrative)
    - A.
    - B.
    - C.
    - D.

EXAMINING PARAGRAPHS OF PROCESS ANALYSIS

Student Writer

Pupusas, Salvadoran Delight

Patty Serrano

We all have at least one kind of food that reminds us of childhood, something that has filled our bellies in time of hunger and perhaps comforted our minds in times of stress. For Patty Serrano, a community college student living at home, that special dish is pupusas. *In El Salvador these are a favorite item in homes and restaurants and at roadside stands. In Southern California, they're available in little restaurants called* pupusarias.

Topic sentences Every time my mom decides to make pupusas, we jump for joy. A pupusa contains

only a few ingredients, and it may sound easy
to make, but really good ones must be made by
experienced hands. My mom is an expert,
having learned as a child from her mother.

Preparation All the ingredients are chosen fresh. The
meat, either pork or beef, can be bought
prepared, but my mom chooses to prepare it
herself. The meat, which is called

Steps

1 "carnitas," is ground and cooked with
tomatoes and spices. The cheese—she uses a
white Jalisco—has to be stringy because that
kind gives pupusas a very good taste,
appearance, and texture. Then comes the

2 preparation of the "masa," or cornmeal. It
has to be soft but not so soft that it falls
apart in the making and handling. All of this
is done while the "comal," or skillet, is

3 being heated. She then grabs a chunk of masa
and forms it into a tortilla like a magician
turning a ball into a thin pancake. Next she

4 grabs small chunks of meat and cheese and
places them in the middle of the tortilla.

5 The tortilla is folded in half and formed
again. After placing the pupusa into the

6 sizzling skillet with one hand, she is
already starting another pupusa. It's amazing
how she does two things at the same time. She

7 turns the pupusas over and over again until

she is sure that <u>they are done.</u> We watch, mouths open, plates empty. In my family it is a tradition that I get the first pupusa because I like them so much. I love opening the hot pupusas, smelling the aroma, and seeing the stringy cheese stretching in the middle. I'm as discriminating as a wine taster. But I never eat a pupusa without "curtido," chopped cabbage with jalapeño. Those items balance the richness of the other

Concluding sentences   ingredients. <u>I could eat Mom's pupusas</u> <u>forever. I guess it has something to do with</u> <u>the way my mom makes them, with experienced,</u> <u>magical, loving hands</u>.

PROFESSIONAL WRITER

The Birth of an Island

Rachel Carson

We usually think of birth in a biological sense, but Rachel Carson describes a different kind—a geological birth. It requires no coach, no midwife, no obstetrician. And unless you can live for thousands or even millions of years, you can't witness the whole process. Nevertheless, it is a process, and it can be described in steps.

1   The birth of a volcanic island is an event marked by prolonged and violent travail: the forces of the earth striving to create, and all the forces of the sea opposing. The sea floor, where an island begins, is probably nowhere more than about fifty miles thick—a thin covering over the vast bulk of the earth. In it are deep cracks and fissures, the results of unequal cooling and shrinkage in past ages. Along such lines of weakness the molten lava from the earth's interior presses up and finally bursts forth into the sea. But a submarine volcano is different from a terrestrial eruption, where lava, molten rocks,

gases, and other ejecta are hurled into the air through an open crater. Here on the bottom of the ocean the volcano has been resisting all the weight of the ocean water above it. Despite the immense pressure of, it may be, two or three miles of sea water, the new volcanic cone builds upward toward the surface in flow after flow of lava. Once within reach of the waves, its soft ash and tuff are violently attacked, and for a long period the potential island may remain a shoal, unable to emerge. But, eventually, in new eruptions, the cone is pushed up into the air and a rampart against the attacks of the waves is built of hardened lava.

EXERCISE 1

1. What type of process analysis (informative or directive) is used in "Birth of an Island"?

2. For what type of audience (well informed, moderately informed, or poorly informed on the topic) is Carson writing?

3. Underline four transitional terms used in this paragraph.

PRACTICING PATTERNS OF PROCESS ANALYSIS

▌ EXERCISE 2

Refer to the paragraph on page 165. Fill in the blanks to complete the process analysis; the analysis is informative but can be taken as directive (as it appears here).

"Pupusas, Salvadoran Delight"

   I. Preparation

      A. Ingredients fresh

      B. Meat either beef or pork

  II. Steps

      A. _____

      B. _____

      C. _____

      D. _____

      E. _____

      F. _____

      G. _____

▌ EXERCISE 3

Refer to the paragraph on page 67. Fill in the blanks to complete the informative process analysis.

"The Birth of an Island"

   I. Background or context

      A. Sea floor

      B. Cracks in surface

  II. Change or development

      A. _____

      B. Cone builds toward surface

C. _____

D. _____

TOPICS FOR PARAGRAPHS OF PROCESS ANALYSIS

Reading-Related Topics

1. *"Pupusas:* Salvadoran Delight": Write about a special food pre-pared in your family now or in your childhood. The food could be your favorite dish, or it might be a treat prepared for a special holiday.
2. "The Birth of an Island": Use this paragraph as a guide to writing about the formation of something else in nature. You could write about a geographical feature such as an alluvial plain, a beach, a lake, a mountain, a desert, or a delta. Or you could write about something from the field of chemistry, biology, or astronomy. For specific information or terminology, refer to general sources such as encyclopedias or introductory textbooks, but be sure to use your own sentences to write the paragraph.

Career-Related Topics

3. Explain how to display, package, sell, or demonstrate a product.
4. Explain how to perform a service or to repair or install a product.
5. Explain the procedure for operating a machine, computer, piece of equipment, or other device.
6. Explain how to manufacture, construct, or cook something.

General Topics

Most of the topics below are directive as they are phrased. However, each can be transformed into a "how-it-was-done" informative topic by personalizing it and explaining stage by stage how you, someone else, or a group did something. For example, you could write either a directive process analysis about how to deal with an obnoxious person or an informative process analysis about how you or someone else dealt with an obnoxious person. Keep in mind that the two types of process analysis are often blended, especially in the personal approach. Many of the following topics will be more interesting to you and your readers if they are personalized.

Most of the topics require some narrowing to be treated in a paragraph. For example, writing about playing baseball is too broad; writing about how to throw a curve ball may be manageable.

7. How to end a relationship without hurting someone's feelings

8. How to pass a test for a driver's license

9. How to get a job at _____

10. How to eat _____

11. How to perform a magic trick

12. How to repair _____

13. How to assemble _____

14. How to learn about another culture

15. How to approach someone you would like to know better

WRITER'S GUIDELINES AT A GLANCE: PROCESS ANALYSIS

1. Decide whether your process analysis is mainly directive or informative, and be appropriately consistent in using pronouns and other designations:

   - For the directive analysis, use the second person, addressing the reader as *you*. The *you* may be understood, even if it is not written.
   - For the informative analysis, use
     a. the first person, speaking as *I* or *we*, or
     b. the third person, speaking about the subject as *he, she, it,* or *they,* or by name.

2. Consider using these basic forms.

Directive	**Informative**
I. Preparation	I. Background or context
A.	A.
B.	B.
II. Steps	II. Change or development
A.	A.
B.	B.
C.	C.

3. In explaining the stages and using technical terms, take into account whether your audience will be mainly well informed, moderately informed, or poorly informed.

4. Use transitional words indicating time or other progression (such as *first, second, then, soon, now, next, after, before, when, finally, at last, therefore, consequently,* and—especially for the informative process analysis—words that show passage of time, such as hours, days of the week, and so on).

5. Avoid recipe language; in other words, do not drop *the, a, an,* or *of.*

8

Cause and Effect: Determining Reasons and Outcomes

WRITING PARAGRAPHS OF CAUSE AND EFFECT

Cause-and-effect relationships are common in our daily lives. A single situation may raise questions about both causes and effects:

> The car won't start. Why? (cause)
>
> What now? (effect)

In a paragraph, you will probably concentrate on either causes or effects, though you may mention both of them. Because you cannot write about all causes or all effects, you should try to identify and develop the most important ones. Consider that some causes are immediate, others remote; some visible, others hidden. Any one or a group of causes can be the most important. The effects of an event can also be complicated. Some may be immediate, others long-range. The sequence of events is not necessarily related to causation. For example, *B* (inflation) may follow *A* (the election of a president), but that sequence does not mean that *A* caused *B*.

Organizing Cause and Effect

One useful approach to developing a cause-or-effect analysis is *listing*. Write down the event, situation, or trend you are concerned about. Then on the left side, list the causes and on the right side list the effects. Looking at the two lists, determine the best side (causes or effects) for your study.

| | **Event, Situation,** | |
Causes	**or Trend**	**Effects**
Bad habits		Financial problems
In-law problems		Liberation
Religious differences		Financial success
Career decision		Safety
Personal abuse	*Divorce*	New relationships
Infidelity		Social adjustment
Sexual incompatibility		Vocational choice
Politics		Problems for children
Money		Independence

First, evaluate the items on your list. Keep in mind that one cause, such as personal abuse, may have its own (remote, hidden, or underlying) cause or partial cause: frustration over job loss, mental problems, tumor on the brain, drug addiction, bad parenting, or weak character. In single paragraphs, one usually deals with immediate causes, such as in-law problems, money, and personal abuse. (These same principles can be applied to effects.)

After you have evaluated the items on your list, choose two or three of the most important causes or effects and proceed.

The causes could be incorporated into a *topic sentence* and then developed in an *outline.*

The main causes of my divorce were in-law problems, money, and personal abuse.

I. In-law problems
   A. Helped too much
   B. Expected too much
II. Money
   A. Poor management
   B. Low-paying job
III. Personal abuse
   A. Verbal
   B. Physical

Your paragraph will derive its structure from either causes or effects, though both causes and effects may be mentioned. Give emphasis and continuity to your writing by repeating key words, such as *cause, reason, effect, result, consequence,* and *outcome.*

The basic structure of your paragraph will look like this:

Topic sentence
Cause or Effect 1
Cause or Effect 2
Cause or Effect 3

EXAMINING PARAGRAPHS OF CAUSE AND EFFECT

Student Writer

A Divorce with Reasons

Sarah Bailey

A few years have passed, and student Sarah Bailey can look back on her divorce and sort out the causes and effects of her failed marriage. This paragraph, which focuses on three main causes, was developed through the listing and outlining shown on pages 73 and 74.

I was married for almost five years. The first year was great, but each of the last four was worse than the previous one.

Topic sentence — The marriage was made in carefree leisure, and the divorce was made in a reality that just got colder and colder. Our first problem

Support (cause) — was the in-laws, actually his parents: mine live in another state, and we saw them only once a year. It was nothing deliberate. His parents wanted to help, and that was the problem. They expected me to be the daughter they never had and him to be a successful businessman and homeowner. They expected too much from both of us, and we couldn't make our own choices. That cause was related to

Support (cause) another one—<u>money.</u> Both of us had low-level jobs in industry. We were around people who were wealthy, but we couldn't buy, belong, and participate as we wanted to. Then I started getting more promotions than he. Finally, he quit his job just at the beginning of a recession, and he couldn't get another one. I told him I would be patient, but at times I was resentful that I was the only one working. As he became more and more frustrated, he started losing his temper with

Support (cause) me and said things that <u>hurt</u> my feelings. One day he hit me. He said he was sorry and even cried, but I could not forgive him. We got a

Concluding sentence divorce. <u>It took me a while before I could look back and see what the causes really were, but by then it was too late to make any changes.</u>

PROFESSIONAL WRITER

What Happens to Steroid Studs?

Anastasia Toufexis

1   *Young men take steroids because they want the Rambo look. However, as* Time *magazine writer Toufexis points out, they get much more than muscles in their steroids-effects package—and what they get, no one wants.*

Drug-enhanced physiques are a hazardous bargain. Steroids can cause temporary acne and balding, upset hormonal production and damage the heart and kidneys. Doctors suspect they may contribute to liver cancer and atherosclerosis. Teens, who are already undergoing physical and psychological stresses, may run some enhanced risks. The drugs can stunt growth by accelerating bone maturation. Physicians also speculate that the chemicals may compromise youngsters' still developing reproductive systems. Steroid users have experienced a shrinking of the testicles and impotence. Dr. Richard Dominguez, a sports specialist in suburban Chicago, starts his lectures to youths with a surefire attention grabber: "You want to shrink your balls? Take steroids." Just as worrisome is the threat to mental health. Drug users are prone to moodiness, depression, irritability and what are known as "roid rages." Ex-user Darren Allen Chamberlain, 26, of Pasadena, Calif., describes himself as an "easy-going guy" before picking up steroids at age 16. Then he turned into a teen Terminator.

▌ EXERCISE 1

1. What is the subject (a situation, circumstance, or trend) at the center of the discussion of steroids?

2. Is this paragraph concerned more with causes, effects, or a combination of both?

3. List five of the effects of steroid use.

PRACTICING PATTERNS OF CAUSE AND EFFECT

▌ EXERCISE 2

Fill in the blanks to complete first the causes outline and then the effects outline.

1. Causes for immigrating to the United States

    I. Desire for a better education
    II. _____
    III. _____
    IV. _____

2. Effects of getting adequate exercise

    I. Muscle tone
    II. _____
    III. _____
    IV. _____

TOPICS FOR PARAGRAPHS OF CAUSE AND EFFECT

Reading-Related Topics

1. "A Divorce with Reasons": Write a paragraph about the effects of a divorce on someone you know, either a divorced person or a relative of a divorced person.
2. Write about the causes for or effects of the good marriage of a couple you know.
3. "What Happens to Steroid Studs?": Write a paragraph about the causes for or effects of steroid use in connection with someone you know.
4. Write about the causes for the use of another drug or substance, such as tobacco, heroin, cocaine, marijuana, LSD, or alcohol— or their effects—in connection with someone you know. Consider including information from a counseling office, health office, library, the American Heart Association, the American Lung Association, or a police station. Pamphlets are readily available.

Career-Related Topics

5. Discuss the effects (benefits) of a particular product or service on the business community, family life, society generally, specific groups (age, income, activities), or an individual.
6. Discuss the needs (thus the cause of development) by individuals, families, or institutions for a particular product or type of product.
7. Discuss the effects of using a certain approach, system, or philosophy in sales, personnel management, or customer service.

General Topics

8. Write a paragraph about the causes of crime (for one individual involved in crime); unemployment (one person who is out of work); leaving home (one person who has left home); emigrating (one person or family); poverty (one person who is poor); school dropout (one person); going to college (one who did); or the success of a product or program on television (one).
9. Write a paragraph about the effects of disease (a particular disease, perhaps on just one person); fighting (one or two people involved in a dispute); fire (a particular one); alcoholism (a certain alcoholic); getting a job (a person with a particular job); early marriage (a person who married very young); teenage parenthood (one person or a couple); or dressing a certain way (one person and his or her style).

WRITER'S GUIDELINES AT A GLANCE:
CAUSE AND EFFECT

1. Have your purpose clearly in mind.
2. Be sure that you have sufficient knowledge of the subject to develop it.
3. Distinguish clearly between causes and effects by using three columns. From your lists select only the most relevant causes or effects.

Causes	Situation	Effects

4. Concentrate primarily on either causes or effects. It is all right to refer to both causes and effects, but only one should provide the framework for your writing.
5. Do not conclude that something is an effect merely because it follows something else.
6. Emphasize your main concern, cause or effect, by repeating key words such as *cause, reason, effect, result, consequence,* and *outcome.*

9

Classification: Establishing Groups

WRITING PARAGRAPHS OF CLASSIFICATION

To explain by classification, you put persons, places, things, or ideas into groups or classes based on their characteristics. Whereas analysis by division deals with the characteristics of just one unit, classification deals with more than one unit, so the subject is plural.

To classify efficiently, try following this procedure:

1. Select a plural subject.
2. Decide on a principle for grouping the units of your subject.
3. Establish the groups, or classes.
4. Write about the classes.

Selecting a Subject

When you say you have different kinds of neighbors, friends, teachers, bosses, or interests, you are classifying; that is, you are forming groups.

In naming the different kinds of people in your neighborhood, you might think of different groupings of your neighbors, the units. For example, some neighbors are friendly, some are meddlesome, and some are private. Some neighbors have yards like Japanese gardens, some have yards like neat but cozy parks, and some have yards like abandoned lots. Some neighbors are affluent, some are comfortable, and some are struggling. Each of these sets is a classification system and could be the focus of a paragraph.

Using a Principle to Avoid Overlapping

All the sets in the preceding section are sound because each group is based on a single concern: neighborly involvement, appearance of

81

the yard, or wealth. This one concern, or controlling idea, is called the *principle*. For example, the principle of neighborly involvement controls the grouping of neighbors into three classes: friendly, meddlesome, and private.

All the classes in any one group must adhere to the controlling principle for that group. You would not say, for example, that your neighbors can be classified as friendly, meddlesome, private, and affluent, because the first three classes relate to neighborly involvement, but the fourth, relating to wealth, refers to another principle. Any one of the first three—the friendly, meddlesome, and private—might also be affluent. The classes should not overlap in this way. Also, every member should fit into one of the available classes.

Establishing Classes

As you name your classes, rule out easy, unimaginative phrasing such as *fast/medium/slow, good/average/bad,* and *beautiful/ordinary/ugly.* Look for creative, original phrases and unusual perspectives.

> *Subject:* neighbors
> *Principle:* neighborhood involvement
> *Classes:* friendly, meddlesome, private

> *Subject:* neighbors
> *Principle:* yard upkeep
> *Classes:* immaculate, neat, messy

> *Subject:* neighbors
> *Principle:* wealth
> *Classes:* affluent, comfortable, struggling

Using Simple and Complex Forms

Classification can take two forms: simple and complex. The *simple* form does not go beyond main divisions in its groupings.

> *Subject:* Neighbors
> *Principle:* Involvement
> *Classes:*   I. Friendly
>   II. Meddlesome
>   III. Private

Complex classifications are based on one principle and then subgrouped by another related principle. The following example classifies neighbors by their neighborly involvement. It then sub-groups two of the classes on the basis of motive.

I. Friendly
II. Meddlesome
   A. Controlling
   B. Emotionally needy
III. Private
   A. Shy
   B. Snobbish
   C. Secretive

EXAMINING PARAGRAPHS OF CLASSIFICATION

Student Writer

Doctors Have Their Symptoms Too

Boris Belinsky

Drawing on his own experiences and those of his family, student Boris Belinsky groups doctors according to their motives.

Because I come from a large family that unfortunately has had a lot of illnesses, I have learned to classify doctors according to

Topic sentence why they became doctors. As doctors can diagnose illnesses by the symptoms they identify, I can figure out doctors' motives by their symptoms, by which I mean behavior. Some doctors have chosen the field of

Support (class) medicine because they want to make money. They hurry their patients (customers) through their multiple office spaces, answering few questions, and never sitting down. Although slow to answer the desperate phone calls, they're fast with the bills. The second class

**Support
(class)**   is the group with <u>scientific</u> interests. Not

as much concerned about money, they're often

found in university hospitals where they

teach and work on special medical problems.

They may be a bit remote and explain symptoms

in technical terms. The third group is my

favorite: those who became doctors to <u>help</u>

**Support
(class)**   <u>people.</u> They spend much time with patients,

often practice in areas that are not

affluent, advocate preventative methods, and

**Concluding
sentence**   do volunteer work. <u>Not all doctors easily</u>

<u>fall into these three groups, but virtually</u>

<u>every one has a tendency to do so.</u>

PROFESSIONAL WRITER

Nobles, Peasants, and Clergy

T. Walter Wallbank

In this passage taken from The Story of Civilization, *historian T. Walter Wallbank classifies medieval society (A.D. 456–1453) into three groups.*

1   Though at times there was considerable social mobility, medieval society conventionally consisted of three classes: the nobles, the peasants, and the clergy. Each of these groups had its own task to perform. Since the vassals [land owners] usually gave military service to their lord in return for their fiefs [estates], the nobles were primarily fighters, belonging to an honored society distinct from the peasant people. . . . In an age of physical violence, society obviously would accord first place to the man with the sword rather than to the man with the hoe. The peasants were the workers; attached to the manors, they produced the crops and did all the menial labor. The Church drew on both the noble and the peasant classes for the clergy. Although the higher churchmen held land as vassals under the feudal system, the clergy formed a class which was considered separate from the nobility and peasantry.

1. Which is the topic sentence in "Nobles, Peasants, and Clergy"?

2. Into what classes does Wallbank break down his subject?

3. What principle does Wallbank use as a basis for classifying members of society?

PRACTICING PATTERNS OF CLASSIFICATION

Fill in the blanks to identify the classes that could be discussed for each subject.

1. Subject: community college students
   Principle: why they attend college
   Classes:

   I. Specialty needs (to take specific courses)

   II. _____

   III. _____

2. Subject: romantic dates
   Principle: characterized by behavior similar to that of aquatic animals

Classes:

   I. Sharks

  II. _____

 III. _____

 IV. _____

Topics for Paragraphs of Classification

Reading-Related Topics

1. "Doctors Have Their Symptoms Too": Classify another vocational group (clergy, teachers, lawyers, police officers, shop owners) according to their reasons for selecting their field.
2. "Nobles, Peasants, and Clergy": In a paragraph, discuss contemporary social classes in a particular community, region, or country.
3. Using Wallbank's paragraph as a model, write about the divisions within a particular company (such as management, sales, manufacturing, distribution) or a particular school (such as administration, faculty, support staff). Name the company or school.

Career-Related Topics

4. Discuss the different types of managers you have encountered (democratic, authoritarian, authoritative, autocratic, buddylike, aloof).
5. Discuss the different types of customers with whom you have dealt (perhaps according to their purpose for seeking your services or products).
6. Discuss the different types of employees you have observed.
7. Discuss the different qualities of products or services in a particular field.

General Topics

Select one of the following groups and decide on a principle for classifying the members. For example, *laughs* might be grouped according to reasons for laughing.

8. Liars	16. Home computers
9. Summer Jobs	17. Churchgoers
10. Coworkers	18. Laughs
11. Houses	19. TV watchers
12. Parks	20. Parties
13. Neighborhoods	21. Mail
14. Motorcycles	22. Music
15. Pet owners	

WRITER'S GUIDELINES AT A GLANCE: CLASSIFICATION

1. Follow this procedure for writing paragraphs of classification:

   - Select a plural subject.
   - Decide on a principle for grouping the units of the subject.
   - Establish the classes (groups).
   - Write about the classes.

2. Avoid uninteresting phrases for your classes, such as *good/average/bad*, *fast/medium/slow*, and *beautiful/ordinary/ugly*.
3. Avoid overlapping classes.
4. Use the writing process to help you arrange your material systematically.
5. Use Roman numeral headings to indicate classes.

     I. Class one
    II. Class two
   III. Class three

6. If you use subclasses, clearly indicate the different levels.
7. Following your outline or outline alternative, give somewhat equal (whatever is appropriate) space to each class.

10

Comparison and Contrast: Showing Similarities and Differences

WRITING PARAGRAPHS OF COMPARISON AND CONTRAST

Comparison and contrast is a method of showing similarities and dissimilarities between subjects. *Comparison* is concerned with organizing and developing points of similarity; *contrast* has the same function for dissimilarity. Sometimes a writing assignment may require that you cover only similarities or only dissimilarities. Occasionally, an instructor may ask you to separate one from the other. Usually, you will combine them in a paragraph. For convenience, the term *comparison* is often applied to both comparison and contrast, because both use the same techniques and are usually combined into one operation.

Generating Topics and Working with the 4 P's

Comparison and contrast is basic to your thinking. In your daily activities, you consider similarities and dissimilarities among persons, things, concepts, political leaders, doctors, friends, instructors, schools, nations, classes, movies, and so on. You naturally turn to comparison and contrast to solve problems and to make decisions in your affairs and in your writing. Because you have had so many comparative experiences, finding a topic to write about is likely to be only a matter of choosing from a great number of appealing ideas. Freewriting, brainstorming, and clustering will help you generate topics that are especially workable and appropriate for particular assignments.

Many college writing assignments will specify a topic or ask you to choose one from a list. Regardless of the source of your topic, the procedure for developing your ideas by comparison and contrast is the same as the procedure for developing topics of your own choosing. That procedure can be appropriately called the "4 *P's*": *purpose, points, patterns,* and *presentation.*

Purpose

Are you trying to show relationships (how things are similar and dissimilar) or to show that one side is better (ranking)? If you want to show that one actor, one movie, one writer, one president, one product, or one idea is better than another, your purpose is to persuade. You will emphasize the superiority of one side over the other in your topic sentence and in your support.

If you want to explain something about a topic by showing each subject in relationship with others, then your purpose is informative. For example, you might be comparing two composers, Beethoven and Mozart. Both were musical geniuses, so you then decide it would be senseless to argue that one is superior to the other. Instead, you choose to reveal interesting information about both by showing them in relation to each other.

Or let's say you have been watching two fathers on television reruns: Bill Cosby as Dr. Cliff Huxtable on "The Cosby Show" and Al Bundy on "Married with Children." Your purpose might again be to show relationships, not to argue that one is better.

Points

Continuing with the example on TV dads, you would come up with a list of ideas, or points you could apply somewhat equally to the two sides. From the list you would select two or three and circle them.

(family members)

(attitude toward family)

position in community

(judgment in solving family problems)

social background

Patterns

Then you would need to organize your material. There are two basic patterns: subject-by-subject and point-by-point. The **subject-**

by-subject pattern presents all of one side and then all of the other.

I. Dr. Cliff Huxtable
   A. Family members
   B. His attitude toward family
   C. His judgment in solving family problems
II. Al Bundy
   A. Family members
   B. His attitude toward family
   C. His judgment in solving family problems

The **point-by-point** pattern shows the points in relation to the sides (subjects) one at a time. This is the more common pattern.

I. Family members
   A. Dr. Cliff Huxtable
      1. Details
      2. Details
   B. Al Bundy
      1.
      2.
II. Attitude toward family
   A. Dr. Cliff Huxtable
      1.
      2.
   B. Al Bundy
      1.
      2.
III. Judgment in solving family problems
   A. Dr. Cliff Huxtable
      1.
      2.
   B. Al Bundy
      1.
      2.

Presentation

Here you would use your outline (or cluster or list) to begin writing your paragraph. You would use appropriate explanations, details, and examples for support.

EXAMINING PARAGRAPHS OF COMPARISON AND CONTRAST

Student Writer

Different TV Dads

Eric Martin

Student Eric Martin, who provided the material for the list and outlines in this chapter, selected the point-by-point pattern for his paragraph.

Cliff Huxtable from "The Bill Cosby Show" and Al Bundy from "Married with Children" are both dads, but the similarity ends with that

Topic sentence biological fact. Whether the television viewer sees these dads in relation to their family members, attitudes toward the family, or judgment in solving family problems, the

I. Family members two dads face each other as opposites, standing more than channels apart. Each one

A. Cliff does have a complete family—wife and children. Cliff has a wife who is charming, stylish, loving, and loyal, and his children

B. Al are lovable, agreeable, and kind. Al Bundy is not so fortunate. His brood is contentious,

II. Attitude toward family self-centered, and mean-minded. Both dads have an appropriate attitude toward their

A. Cliff family. Cliff is affectionate to his wife and protective of his family. He believes that he is there to share with his wife and to nurture his children, so he gives quality and

B. Al quantity time. Al has a different situation

(perhaps one he deserves); he must deal with a lazy, self-serving wife, whose idea of loveliness is a gold lamé miniskirt, a see-through blouse, and four-inch spike heels—in the kitchen. His sluttish daughter and delinquent son give him a hard time, and he returns it, if possible. Of course, <u>both dads</u> <u>have family problems to solve.</u> <u>Cliff</u> helps his family cleverly with problems big and small. Whether a goldfish has died or the children are torn between conflicting values, Dad is there with guidance and jokes. <u>Al</u> is also there when problems arise, but the guidance is nonexistent, and the jokes are mostly on him. The family comes to him mainly for money, and he never has enough. Oddly, both families seem to work, one on the basis of love, the other on the basis of self-interest. <u>In each</u> <u>instance, we viewers (who will be seeing them</u> <u>in reruns forever) can safely say that the</u> <u>family members deserve each other.</u>

III. Judgment in solving family problems

A. Cliff

B. Al

Concluding sentence

Professional Writer

Pink Kittens and Blue Spaceships

Alison Lurie

What are the sources of gender identity? In this passage from her book The Language of Clothes, *Alison Lurie shows that people condition children from birth.*

1   In early childhood girls' and boys' clothes are often identical in cut and fabric, as if in recognition of the fact that their bodies

are much alike. But the T-shirts, pull-on slacks and zip jackets intended for boys are usually made in darker colors (especially forest green, navy, red and brown) and printed with designs involving sports, transportation and cute wild animals. Girls' clothes are made in paler colors (especially pink, yellow and green) and decorated with flowers and cute domestic animals. The suggestion is that the boy will play vigorously and travel over long distances; the girl will stay home and nurture plants and small mammals. Alternatively, these designs may symbolize their wearers: the boy is a cuddly bear or a smiling tiger, the girl a flower or a kitten. There is also a tendency for boys' clothes to be fullest at the shoulders and girls' at the hips, anticipating their adult figures. Boys' and men's garments also emphasize the shoulders with horizontal stripes, epaulets or yokes of contrasting color. Girls' and women's garments emphasize the hips and rear through the strategic placement of gathers and trimmings.

▌ EXERCISE 1

1. Does the paragraph "Pink Kittens and Blue Spaceships" stress comparison or contrast?

2. Is the purpose mainly to inform or persuade, or both?

3. What are the two main points used for comparing and contrasting girls' and boys' clothes?

4. Is the pattern of the piece point by point or subject by subject?

PRACTICING PATTERNS OF COMPARISON AND CONTRAST

EXERCISE 2

Fill in the blanks to complete the comparisons and contrasts in the following outlines.

1. Friends: Marla and Justine

    I. Marla

        A. Appearance

        B. _____

        C. _____

    II. Justine

        A. _____

        B. Personality

        C. _____

2. Two Bosses: Mr. Santo and Ms. Elliott

    I. Disposition

        A. Mr. Santo

        B. Ms. Elliott

    II. Knowledge of _____

        A. _____

        B. Ms. Elliott

    III. _____

        A. Mr. Santo

        B. _____

TOPICS FOR PARAGRAPHS OF COMPARISON AND CONTRAST

Reading-Related Topics

1. "Different TV Dads": Write a paragraph of comparison and contrast about two other television sitcom characters. Consider characters with similar roles on different shows. Characters

with distinctively different behavior, appearance, and reputation usually make the most interesting subjects.

2. Write a paragraph of comparison and contrast about two real-life parents and their families. You might compare and contrast a parent's account of what his or her parent(s) or family was like with what you have experienced.

3. "Pink Kittens and Blue Spaceships": Compare and contrast the toys traditionally given to boys and girls.

4. Compare and contrast the games or recreation generally made available to girls and boys.

Career-Related Topics

5. Compare and contrast two products or services, with the purpose of showing that one is better.

6. Compare and contrast two management styles or two working styles.

7. Compare and contrast two career fields to show that one is better for you.

8. Compare and contrast a public school and a business.

9. Compare and contrast an athletic team and a business.

General Topics

The following topics refer to general subjects. Provide specific names and other detailed information as you develop your ideas by using the 4 *P*'s.

10. Two diets
11. Two fast-food places
12. Two textbooks
13. Two gymnasiums
14. Two careers
15. Two people who play the same sport
16. Two generations
17. Two motorcycles, cars, snowmobiles
18. Two actors, singers, musicians
19. Two ways of learning
20. Two ways of exercising
21. Two kinds of child care
22. Two mothers: one who stays at home and one who works outside the home

WRITER'S GUIDELINES AT A GLANCE:
COMPARISON AND CONTRAST

Work with the 4 *P*'s:

1. Purpose: Decide whether you want to inform (show relationships) or persuade (show that one side is better).
2. Points: Decide which ideas you will apply to each side. Consider beginning by making a list to select from.
3. Patterns: Decide whether to use subject-by-subject or point-by-point organization.
4. Presentation: Decide to what extent you should develop your ideas. Be sure to use cross-references to make connections and to use examples and details to support your views.
5. Your basic subject-by-subject outline will probably look like this:

   I. Subject 1
      A. Point 1
      B. Point 2
   II. Subject 2
      A. Point 1
      B. Point 2

6. Your basic point-by-point outline will probably look like this:

   I. Point 1
      A. Subject 1
      B. Subject 2
   II. Point 2
      A. Subject 1
      B. Subject 2

11

Definition: Clarifying Terms

WRITING PARAGRAPHS OF DEFINITION

Most definitions are short; they consist of a synonym (a word that has the same meaning as the term to be defined), a phrase, or a sentence. For example, we might say that a hypocrite is a person "professing beliefs or virtues he or she does not possess." Terms can also be defined by *etymology*, or word history. *Hypocrite* once meant "actor" (*hypocrites*) in Greek because an actor was pretending to be someone else. We may find this information interesting and revealing, but the history of a word may be of no use because the meaning has changed drastically over the years. Sometimes definitions occupy a paragraph or an entire essay. The short definition is called a *simple definition*; the longer one is known as an *extended definition*.

Techniques for Development

Paragraphs of definition can take many forms. Among the more common techniques for writing a paragraph of definition are the patterns we have worked with in previous chapters. Consider each of those patterns when you need to write an extended definition. For a particular term, some forms will be more useful than others; use the pattern that best fulfills your purpose.

Each of the following questions takes a pattern of writing and directs it toward definition.

- Narration
  Can I tell an anecdote or story to define this subject (such as *jerk, humanitarian, patriot*)? This form may overlap with description and exemplification.

- Description
  Can I describe this subject (such as *a whale* or *the moon*)?

- Exemplification
  Can I give examples of this subject (such as naming individuals to provide examples of *actors, diplomats,* or *satirists*)?

- Analysis by Division
  Can I divide this subject into parts (for example, the parts of a *heart, cell,* or *carburetor*)?

- Process Analysis
  Can I define this subject (such as *lasagna, tornado, hurricane, blood pressure,* or any number of scientific processes) by describing how to make it or how it occurs? (Common to the methodology of communicating in science, this approach is sometimes called the "operational definition.")

- Cause and Effect
  Can I define this subject (such as *a flood, a drought, a riot,* or *a cancer*) by its causes or effects?

- Classification
  Can I group this subject (such as kinds of *families, cultures, religions, governments*) into classes?

Subject	Class	Characteristics
A republic	is a form of government	in which power resides in the people (the electorate).

- Comparison and Contrast
  Can I define this subject (such as *extremist* or *patriot*) by explaining what it is similar to and different from? If you are defining *orangutan* to a person who has never heard of one but has heard of the gorilla, then you could make comparison-and-contrast statements. If you want to define *patriot,* then you might want to stress what it is not (the contrast) before you explain what it is: a patriot is not a one-dimensional flag waver, not someone who hates "foreigners" because America is always right and always best.

When you develop ideas for a definition paragraph, use a cluster to consider all the paragraph patterns you have learned. Put a double bubble around the subject to be defined. Then put a single bubble around the paragraph patterns and add appropriate words. If a paragraph pattern is not relevant to what you are defining, leave it blank. If you want to expand your range of information, you could add a bubble for a simple dictionary definition and another for an etymological definition.

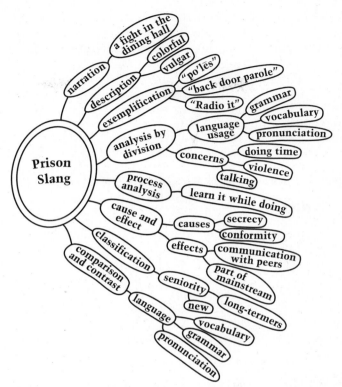

Bubble cluster showing how a term could be defined using different paragraph patterns.

Order

The organization of your extended definition is likely to be one of emphasis, but it may be space or time, depending on the subject material. You may use just one pattern of development for the overall sequence. If so, then you would employ the principles of organization discussed in previous chapters.

Introduction and Development

Consider these ways of introducing a definition: with a question, with a statement of what it is not, with a statement of what it originally meant, or with a discussion of why a clear definition is important. You may use a combination of these ways or all of them before you continue with your definition.

Development, whether in the form of sentences for the paragraph or of paragraphs for the essay, is likely to represent one or more of the patterns of narration, description, exposition (with its own subdivisions), and argumentation.

Whether you personalize a definition depends on your purpose and your audience. Your instructor may ask you to write about a word within the context of your experience or to write about it from a detached, clinical viewpoint.

EXAMINING PARAGRAPHS OF DEFINITION

Student Writer

Going Too Far

Linda Wong

After hearing people say, "I just can't love him [or her] enough," and also "It was too much of a good thing," Linda Wong set out to explore the definition of the word extremist.

What the term does not mean	Some people believe that it is good to be an extremist in some areas, but those people are actually changing the meaning of the
Simple definition	word. According to the <u>Random House Dictionary of the English Language,</u> the word extremism itself means "excessively biased
Topic sentence	ideas, intemperate conduct." <u>The extremist goes too far; that means going too far in whatever the person is doing.</u> I once heard
Example/ Contrast	someone say that it is good for people to be extremists in love. But that is not true. <u>It is good to be enthusiastically and sincerely in love, but extremists in love love</u>

excessively and intemperately. People who
love well may be tender and sensitive and
attentive, but extremists are possessive or
smothering. The same can be said of parents.

**Example/
Contrast**   We all want good parents, but parental
extremists involve themselves too much in the
lives of their children, who, in turn, may
find it difficult to develop as individuals
and become independent. Even in patriotism,
good patriots are to be distinguished from

**Example/
Contrast**   extreme patriots. Good patriots love their
country, but extreme patriots love their
country so much that they think citizens from
other countries are inferior and suspect.
Extreme patriots may have Hitler-like
tendencies. Just what is wrong with
extremists then? It is the loss of

Examples   perspective. The extremists are so
preoccupied with one concern that they lose
their sense of balance. They are the
workaholics, the zealots, the superpatriots
of the world. They may begin with a good
objective, but they focus on it so much that
they can become destructive, obnoxious, and

**Effect and
Concluding
sentence**   often pitiful. The worst effect is that these
extremists lose their completeness as human
beings.

PROFESSIONAL WRITER

Tornado

Morris Tepper

A tornado may be identified as a particular kind of whirling, highly destructive windstorm. Morris Tepper extends his definition so that readers will have a good understanding of the many facets of this phenomenon.

What exactly is a tornado? The general picture is familiar enough. The phenomenon is usually brewed on a hot, sticky day with south winds and an ominous sky. From the base of a thundercloud a funnel-shaped cloud extends a violently twisting spout toward the earth. As it sucks in matter in its path, the twister may turn black, brown or occasionally even white (over snow). The moving cloud shows an almost continuous display of sheet lightning. It lurches along in a meandering path, usually northeastward, at 25 to 40 miles per hour. Sometimes it picks up its finger from the earth for a short distance and then plants it down again. The funnel is very slender: its wake of violence generally averages no more than 400 yards wide. As the tornado approaches, it is heralded by a roar of hundreds of jet planes or thousands of railroad cars. Its path is a path of total destruction. Buildings literally explode as they are sucked by the tornado's low-pressure vortex (where the pressure drop is as much as 10 percent) and by its powerful whirling winds (estimated at up to 500 miles per hour). The amount of damage depends mainly on whether the storm happens to hit populated areas. The worst tornado on record in the U.S. was one that ripped across Missouri, lower Illinois and Indiana in three hours on March 18, 1925, and killed 689 people. The tornado's lifetime is as brief as it is violent. Within a few tens of miles (average: about 16 miles) it spends its force and suddenly disappears.

EXERCISE 1

1. Which sentence in "Tornado" carries the most basic definition?

2. Which two paragraph patterns are used throughout this definition?

3. Which pattern is used more?

PRACTICING PATTERNS OF DEFINITION

EXERCISE 2

Fill in the double bubble with a term to be defined. You might want to define a term like *culturally diverse society, educated person, leader, role model, friend, puppy love, true love, success,* or *intelligence.* Then fill in at least one more bubble on the right for each paragraph pattern. If the pattern does not apply (that is, if it would not provide useful information for your definition), mark it NA ("not applicable").

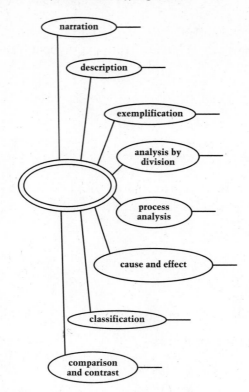

TOPICS FOR PARAGRAPHS OF DEFINITION

Reading-Related Topics

1. "Going Too Far": Apply the definition of *extremist* from Linda Wong's paragraph to a situation you are familiar with: an over-protective parent; a controlling companion; an overly control-ling boss; a too-strict police officer or teacher; a too-virtuous friend; a preacher; a too-clean housekeeper (companion, parent); a zealous patriot; a person fanatical about a diet; a person con-cerned too much with good health or exercise. You might begin your paragraph with the statement: "It is good to be _____, but when _____ is car-ried to the extreme, the result is _____."

2. "Tornado": Define another natural disaster, such as a flood, hurricane, drought, dust storm, or earthquake.

3. Define a natural process, such as oxidation, erosion, photosyn-thesis, or digestion.

Career-Related Topics

4. Define one of the following terms by using the appropriate pattern(s) of development (such as exemplification, cause and effect, narration, comparison and contrast): *total quality management, quality control, downsizing, outsourcing, business ethics, customer satisfaction, cost effectiveness.*

General Topics

Write a paragraph of extended definition about one of these terms.

5. Workaholic	13. Politician
6. Sexist	14. Liberated woman
7. Sexual harassment	15. Hacker
8. Macho	16. Fast food
9. Soul food	17. Rap music
10. Rock music	18. Street smart
11. Common sense	19. Greed
12. Family	20. Ecology

WRITER'S GUIDELINES AT A GLANCE: DEFINITION

1. Use clustering to consider other patterns of development that may be used to define your term.

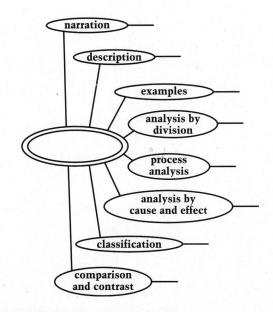

2. The organization of your extended definition is likely to be one of emphasis, but it may be space or time, depending on the subject material. You may use just one pattern of development for the overall organization.

3. Consider these ways of introducing a definition: with a question, with a statement of what it is not, with a statement of what it originally meant, or with a discussion of why a clear definition is important. You may use a combination of these ways before you continue with your definition.

4. Whether you personalize a definition depends on your purpose and your audience. Your instructor may ask you to write about a word within the context of your own experience or to write about it from a detached, clinical viewpoint.

12

Argument: Writing to Influence

WRITING PARAGRAPHS OF ARGUMENT

Persuasion and Argument Defined

Persuasion is a broad term. When we persuade, we try to influence people to think in a certain way or to do something. *Argument* is persuasion on a topic about which reasonable people disagree. Argument involves controversy. Whereas exercising appropriately is probably not controversial because reasonable people do not dispute the idea, an issue such as gun control is. In this chapter we will be concerned mainly with the kind of persuasion that involves argument.

Components of Your Paragraph

Statements of argument are informal or formal in design. An opinion column in a newspaper is likely to have little set structure, whereas an argument in college writing is likely to be tightly organized. Nevertheless, the opinion column and the college paper have much in common. Both provide a proposition, which is the main point of the argument, and both provide support, which is the evidence or the reasons that back up the proposition.

For a well-structured paragraph, an organizational plan is desirable. Consider these elements when you write a paragraph of argument, and ask yourself the following questions as you develop your ideas.

> *Background:* What is the historical or social context for this controversial issue?
>
> *Proposition* (the *topic sentence* of a paragraph of argument): What do I want my audience to believe or do?

Qualification of proposition: Can I limit my proposition so that those who disagree cannot easily challenge me with exceptions? If, for example, I am in favor of using animals for scientific experimentation, am I concerned only with medical experiments or with any use, including that pertaining to the cosmetic industry?

Refutation (taking the opposing view into account, mainly to point out its fundamental weakness): What is the view on the other side, and why is it flawed in reasoning and/or evidence?

Support: In addition to sound reasoning, can I use appropriate facts, examples, statistics, and opinions of authorities?

The basic form for a paragraph of argument includes the proposition (the topic sentence) and support. The support sentences are, in effect, *because* statements; that is, the proposition is valid *because* of the support. Your organization should look something like this.

Proposition (topic sentence): It is time to pass a national law restricting smoking in public places.

    I. Discomfort of the nonsmoker (support 1)
   II. Health of the nonsmoker (support 2)
  III. Cost to the nation (support 3)

Kinds of Evidence

In addition to sound reasoning generally, you can use these kinds of evidence.

First, you can offer facts. Martin Luther King, Jr., was killed in Memphis, Tennessee, on April 4, 1968. Because an event that has happened is true and can be verified, this statement about King is a fact. But that James Earl Ray acted alone in killing King is to some a questionable fact. That King was the greatest of all civil rights leaders is opinion because it cannot be verified.

Some facts are readily accepted because they are general knowledge—you and your reader know them to be true because they can be or have been verified. Other "facts" are based on personal observation and are reported in various publications but may be false or questionable. You should always be concerned about the reliability of the source for both the information you use and the information used by those with other viewpoints. Still other "facts" are genuinely debatable because of their complexity or the incompleteness of the knowledge available.

Second, you can cite examples. You must present a sufficient number of examples, and the examples must be relevant.

Third, you can present statistics. Statistics are facts and data of a numerical kind that are classified and tabulated in order to present significant information about a given subject.

Avoid presenting a long list of figures; select statistics carefully and relate them to things familiar to your reader. The millions of dollars spent on a war in a single week, for example, become more comprehensible when expressed in terms of what the money would purchase in education, highways, or urban renewal.

To test the validity of statistics, either yours or your opponent's, ask: Who gathered them? Under what conditions? For what purpose? How are they used?

Fourth, you can cite evidence from, and opinions of, authorities. Most readers accept facts from recognized, reliable sources—governmental publications, standard reference works, and books and periodicals published by established firms. In addition, they will accept evidence and opinions from individuals who, because of their knowledge and experience, are recognized as experts.

In using authoritative sources as proof, keep these points in mind:

- Select authorities who are generally recognized as experts in their field.
- Use authorities who qualify in the field pertinent to your argument.
- Select authorities whose views are not biased.
- Try to use several authorities.
- Identify an authority's credentials clearly in your paragraph.

EXAMINING PARAGRAPHS OF ARGUMENT

Student Writer

A New Wind Blowing

Eric Miller

Eric Miller isn't asking people to stop smoking; he's asking them only to stop smoking in public places.

One of the most common complaints heard in restaurants and work places pertains to smoking. In all crowded public places, when a smoker lights up, people get upset for

reasons they believe are valid. Along with

Proposition
(topic
sentence)
them, I say it is time to pass a national law

restricting smoking in public places.

Qualification   Reasonable exceptions can be worked out.

Three reasons make this proposition right.

Support 1   One is discomfort. Most people don't like to

Support 2   breathe secondhand smoke. It smells bad. That

reason is coupled with the health reason.

Studies indicate (as reported by Joseph

Califano, former Secretary of Health,

Authoritative
statement
with statistics
Education, and Welfare) that more than 5,000

Americans die each year from secondhand smoke

and that people living with smokers are 80

percent more likely to get lung cancer than

those who do not live with smokers. In 1993

Authoritative
statement
the Environmental Protection Agency formally

classified secondhand smoke as a potent

carcinogen—in a class with asbestos.

Support 3   Connected with this health problem is the

matter of cost. The last five surgeons

general have agreed that secondhand smoke is

a significant health problem, with a huge

cost to society in medical bills and lost job

productivity. Although many smokers concur

Refutation   with the proposal for restriction, others

feel that they would lose their rights. They

shouldn't. They can continue to smoke, but

only if they do not jeopardize the health of

Concluding sentence others in public places. <u>Discomfort, bad</u> <u>health, and bills for taxpayers are too much</u> for society to pay in order to live <u>without</u> <u>restriction.</u>

PROFESSIONAL WRITER

What I Told My Children About Substance Abuse

Joseph A. Califano, Jr.

As president of the National Center on Addiction and Substance Abuse at Columbia University, Joseph A. Califano, Jr., is active in antidrug programs. Here he explains what he told his own children.

1   With all three of my children, I made two points. First, each was a creature of God, blessed with brains and talent. With such generous divine gifts goes a moral obligation to develop those talents and use them to help others less fortunate. That's why it is morally wrong to use drugs. I also told them that alcohol and drugs were two things that could ruin lives, either by leading to an auto accident or by causing addiction. They pointed out that I smoked cigarettes and drank Scotch. My answer: Had I known at age fourteen, when I started smoking, what we learned by the 1970s, I hope I would never have lit up. Today baby-boomer parents who may have smoked pot in college can tell their kids that we know a lot more about marijuana than we did 25 years ago. We know that it can savage short-term memory and that it adversely affects motor skills and inhibits social and emotional development—just at the time such skills and development are most critical, when kids are in school. We can tell them that smoking pot as a young teen is decidedly more dangerous than beginning at twenty something. Our research shows that the earlier someone smokes marijuana, the likelier that youngster is to move on to other drugs. Children who smoke pot before age twelve are 42 times likelier to use drugs like cocaine and heroin than those who first smoked pot after age sixteen.

█ EXERCISE 1

1. Underline the proposition of Califano's argument.
2. The sentence "They [Califano's children] pointed out that I smoked cigarettes and drank Scotch" at first appears to be a rebuttal of Califano's argument. However, it is a false rebuttal. Why is it false?
3. What are three of Califano's arguments against smoking pot?

PRACTICING PATTERNS OF ARGUMENT

█ EXERCISE 2

Fill in the blanks with supporting statements for each proposition. Each outline uses the following pattern:

>   Proposition
>
>   I. Support
>   II. Support
>   III. Support

1. Proposition: College athletes should be paid.

   I. _____

   II. They work long hours in practice and competition.

   III. They have less time than many other students for study.

2. Proposition: Zoos are beneficial institutions.

   I. _____

   II. They preserve endangered species by captive breeding.

   III. They study animal diseases and find cures.

TOPICS FOR PARAGRAPHS OF ARGUMENT

Reading-Related Topics

1. "A New Wind Blowing": Write a paragraph of argument opposing Miller's view.
2. Write a paragraph in support of Miller's view but applied to a specific local or work situation.

3. "What I Told My Children About Substance Abuse": Write a paragraph of argument opposing Califano's view.
4. Write a paragraph of argument in support of Califano's view but with different support.

Career-Related Topics

5. Write a paragraph of argument to convince people that workers at a particular company should or should not be laid off.
6. Write a paragraph of argument to convince people that workers in a particular service industry should or should not go on strike.

General Topics

The following are broad subject areas. You will have to limit your focus for a paragraph of argument. You may also modify the topics to fit specific situations.

7. School dress codes
8. School uniforms
9. Sex education
10. Defining sexual harassment
11. Changing the juvenile justice system
12. Endangered species legislation
13. Advertising tobacco
14. Combatting homelessness
15. State-run lotteries
16. Jury reform
17. Legalizing prostitution
18. Censoring rap and/or rock music
19. Cost of illegal immigration
20. Installation of local traffic signs
21. Foot patrols by local police
22. Change in (your) college registration procedure
23. Local rapid transit
24. Surveillance by video (on campus, in neighborhoods, or in shopping areas)
25. Zone changes for stores selling liquor
26. Curfew for teenagers
27. Laws keeping known gang members out of parks

WRITER'S GUIDELINES AT A GLANCE: ARGUMENT

1. Consider which aspects of the formal argument you need for your paragraph:

   - Background: What is the historical or social context for this controversial issue?
   - Proposition (the *topic sentence*): What do I want my audience to believe or do?
   - Qualification of proposition: Have I limited my proposition so that I cannot be easily challenged with exceptions?
   - Refutation (taking the opposing view into account, mainly to point out its weaknesses): What is the view on the other side, and why is it flawed in reasoning and/or evidence?
   - Support: In addition to sound reasoning, have I used appropriate facts, examples, statistics, and opinions of authorities?

2. The basic pattern of a paragraph of argument is likely to be in this form:

   Proposition (the topic sentence)

      I. Support 1
     II. Support 2
    III. Support 3

13

From Paragraph to Essay

WRITING THE SHORT ESSAY

The definition of a paragraph gives us a framework for defining the essay: A paragraph is a group of sentences, each with the function of supporting a single, main idea, which is contained in the topic sentence.

The main parts of a paragraph are the topic sentence (subject and treatment), support (evidence and reasoning), and, often, the concluding sentence at the end. Now let's use that framework for an essay: An essay is a group of paragraphs, each with the function of stating or supporting a controlling idea called the thesis.

The main parts of the essay are as follows:

Introduction: carries the thesis, which states the controlling idea—much like the topic sentence for a paragraph but on a larger scale.
Development: evidence and reasoning—the support.
Conclusion: an appropriate ending—often a restatement of or reflection on the thesis.

Thus, considered structurally, the paragraph is often an essay in miniature. That does not mean that all paragraphs can grow up to be essays or that all essays can shrink to become paragraphs. For college writing, however, a good understanding of the parallel between well-organized paragraphs and well-organized essays is useful. As you learn the properties of effective paragraphs—those with a strong topic sentence and strong support—you also learn how to organize an essay, if you just magnify the procedure.

The following diagram illustrates the parallel parts of outlines, paragraphs, and essays:

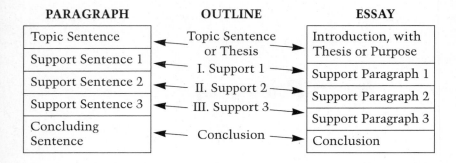

Of course, the parallel components are not exactly the same in a paragraph and an essay. The paragraph is shorter and requires much less development, and some paragraph topics simply couldn't be developed much more extensively to their advantage. But let's consider the ones that can. What happens? How do we proceed?

Introductory Paragraph

The topic sentence idea is expanded to the introductory paragraph through elaboration: explanation, historical background, anecdote, quotation, or stress on the significance of an idea. Usually the introduction is about three to six sentences long. If you say too much, your paper will be top-heavy. If you don't say enough, your readers will be confused. But a solid opening paragraph should

- introduce the subject through the thesis or controlling idea.
- gain reader interest.
- move the reader into the middle paragraphs. You should avoid any statement of apology about your topic or your writing and avoid beginning with a statement like "I am writing an essay about. . . ."

Middle Paragraphs

The middle paragraphs are similar to the paragraphs you have been writing. Each has its own unity based on the topic sentence, moves logically and coherently, and has adequate and appropriate development. The topic sentence is usually at the beginning of the paragraph in a college essay, regardless of the form. Although some essays are an expansion of a particular form of discourse and therefore use basically the same pattern for each paragraph, many essays combine the forms. For example, you might have one middle paragraph that gives examples, one that defines, and one that classifies. You may also have combinations within paragraphs. Nevertheless, the paragraphs are always related to the central idea and presented in a logical arrangement. The coherence of the paragraphs can often be improved by the use of the same principles that you have applied to individual paragraphs: using sequence words such as *first, second,* and *third;* using transitional words such as *therefore, moreover,* and *for example;* and arranging material in chronological order, spatial order, or order of relative importance.

Concluding Paragraph

Like the introductory paragraph, the concluding paragraph is a special unit with a specific function. In the concluding paragraph, usually three to six sentences long, you end on a note of finality. The way that you end depends on what you want to do. If you can't decide on how to end, try going back to your introduction and see what you said there. If you posed a question, the answer should be in the conclusion. If you laid out the framework for an exploration of the topic, then perhaps you will want to bring your discussion together with a summary statement. Or perhaps a quotation, an anecdote, or a restatement of the thesis in slightly different words would be effective. Do not end with a complaint, an apology, or the introduction of a new topic or new support. And do not begin your conclusion with the words such as "last but not least" or "in conclusion." Try for a fresh approach.

EXAMINING A PARAGRAPH AND AN ESSAY

The following paragraph and essay, both on the topic of drunk driving, were written by the same student. Notice how each is developed.

Student Writer

Get Them Off the Road (paragraph)

Daniel Humphreys

Topic sentence

Drunk driving has become such a severe problem in California that something must be done. The best solution is to do what Sweden did long ago: lower the blood-alcohol content level to .04% for drunk-driving arrests.

I. Support <u>Driving</u> is not a right; it <u>is a privilege,</u> and that privilege should not be extended to the person who drinks to the extent that his or her physical and mental abilities are significantly impaired. <u>Alcohol,</u> working as a

II. Support depressant, <u>affects our entire nervous system,</u> according to numerous sources cited in <u>The Police Officer's Source Book.</u> As a result of this impairment, "50 percent of all fatal traffic accidents" involve intoxicated drivers, as reported by the National Highway Traffic Safety Administration. Cavenaugh and Associates, research specialists, say that in California 47,000 people were killed in the five-year period from 1993 through 1997. They

III. Support go on to say that <u>intoxicated drivers cost us somewhere between eleven billion and twenty- four billion dollars each year.</u> <u>It is time to</u>

Concluding <u>give drunk drivers a message:</u> "Stay off the
sentence road. You are costing us pain, injury, and death, and no one has the right to do that."

Get Them Off the Road (essay)

Daniel Humphreys

The state of California, along with the rest of the nation, has a problem with
Introduction society involving drinking and driving.

Thesis of essay

Prohibition is not the answer, as history has demonstrated. But there is a practical answer to be found in a law. <u>I believe that the legal BAC (blood-alcohol concentration) while driving should be lowered from .08 percent to .04 percent for three strong reasons.</u>

Topic sentence of paragraph

I. Support paragraph 1

First, <u>driving in California is a privilege,</u> not a right, and <u>a person impaired by alcohol should not be allowed that privilege.</u> Statutory law states that when stopped by a police officer who suspects drunk driving, one must submit to a BAC test. The level of impairment is an individual trait because of the elapsed time of consumption, body size, and tolerance, but <u>alcohol</u> is a depressant to all of us. It <u>affects our nervous system and slows our muscular reactions.</u> As a result of extensive scientific study, the nation of Sweden determined that .04 percent BAC was the level of significant impairment, and, therefore, it passed a federal law to enforce drunk driving at that point. Penalties there are extreme.

Topic sentence of paragraph

II. Support paragraph 2

<u>We,</u> like the people in Sweden, <u>are</u> concerned about the dangers of drunk driving. The National Highway Traffic Safety Administration has stated that <u>"50 percent of all fatal accidents"</u> involve intoxicated

drivers and that 75 percent of the drivers
have a BAC of .10 percent or greater.
Cavenaugh and Associates, a California think
tank, reports that in the five-year period
between 1993 and 1997, 227,000 people were
injured and 47,000 were killed in alcohol-
related accidents in the state of California.

Topic
sentence of   Even if we are among the fortunate few
paragraph   who are not touched directly by the problems
of drunk driving, there are other effects.

III. Support   One is money. There is the loss of
paragraph 3
production, cost of insurance, cost of delays
in traffic, cost of medical care for those
who have no insurance, and many other costs.
Cavenaugh and Associates say that drunk
drivers cost us somewhere between $11 billion
and $24 billion dollars a year.

Conclusion   Police officers report that drinking
people are quick to say, "I'm okay to drive,"
but in one year alone our nation loses more
lives than it lost in the entire Vietnam War.
To lower the legal BAC limit to .04 percent
Restated
thesis   would mean saving lives, property, and money.

EXERCISE 1

The following paragraph could easily be expanded into an essay because the topic sentence and its related statements can be developed into an introduction; each of the main divisions (five) can be
expanded into a separate paragraph; and the restated topic sentence
can, with elaboration, become the concluding paragraph. Divide the

paragraph below with lines and annotate it in the left-hand margin to show the parts that would be developed further. The topic sentence and its related statements have already been marked for you.

What Is a Gang?

Will Cusak

The word <u>gang</u> is often used loosely to mean "a group of people who go around together," but that does not satisfy the concerns of law enforcement people and sociologists. <u>For these professionals, the definition of gang has five parts.</u> These five parts combine to form a unit. First a gang has to have a name. Some well-known gang names are Bloods, Crips, Hell's Angels, and Mexican Mafia. The second part of the definition is clothing or other identifying items such as tattoos. The clothing may be of specific brands or colors, such as blue for Crips and red for Bloods. Members of the Aryan Brotherhood often have blue thunderbolt tattoos. A third component is rituals. They may involve such things as the use of handshakes, other body language or signing, and graffiti. A fourth is binding membership. A gang member is part of an organization, a kind of family, with obligations and codes of behavior to follow. Finally, a gang will be involved in some criminal behavior, something

Topic sentence with related statements

Introduction

```
such as prostitution, drugs, thievery, or

burglary. There are many different kinds of

gangs—ethnic, regional, behavioral—but they

all have these five characteristics.
```

Topics for Short Essays

Many paragraph topics in this book can become topics for short essays. Look through the lists of "Reading-Related Topics," "Career-Related Topics," and "General Topics" at the end of Chapters 3 through 12 to find ideas that can be expanded. Here are some ways to accomplish the expansion.

> *Narration:* Expand each part of the narrative form (situation, conflict, struggle, outcome, meaning) into one or more paragraphs. Give the most emphasis to the struggle.
>
> *Description:* Expand each unit of descriptive detail into a paragraph. All paragraphs should support the dominant impression.
>
> *Exemplification:* Expand one example into an extended example or expand a group of examples into separate paragraphs. Each paragraph should support the main point.
>
> *Analysis by Division:* Expand your discussion by treating each part of your unit in a separate paragraph.
>
> *Process Analysis:* Expand the preparation and each step in the process into a separate paragraph.
>
> *Cause and Effect:* Expand each cause or effect into a separate paragraph.
>
> *Classification:* Expand each class, or category, into a separate paragraph.
>
> *Comparison and Contrast:* In the point-by-point pattern, expand each point into a separate paragraph.
>
> In the subject-by-subject pattern, first expand each subject into a separate paragraph. If you have sufficient material on each point, you can also expand each point into a separate paragraph.
>
> *Definition:* Expand each aspect of the definition (characteristics, examples, comparative points) into a separate paragraph.
>
> *Argument:* Expand the refutation and each main division of support into a separate paragraph.

Of course, the statement that a paragraph is seldom made up of a single pattern is even more true for the essay. Most essays have a mixture of patterns, though one pattern may prevail and provide the main structure. Therefore, any topic selected from the end-of-chapter suggestions should be developed with an open mind about possibilities of using more than one pattern of development.

WRITER'S GUIDELINES AT A GLANCE: FROM PARAGRAPH TO ESSAY

You do not usually set out to write an essay by first writing a paragraph. But the organization for the paragraph and the essay is often the same, and the writing process is also the same. You still proceed from prewriting to topic, to outline, to draft, to revising, to editing, to final paper. The difference is often only a matter of development and indentation.

1. The well-designed paragraph and the well-designed essay often have the same form.

    a. The introduction carries the thesis, which states the controlling idea—much like the topic sentence for a paragraph but on a larger scale.
    b. The development, or middle part, supplies evidence and reasoning—the support.
    c. The conclusion provides an appropriate ending—often a restatement of, or reflection on, the thesis.

2. These are the important relationships:

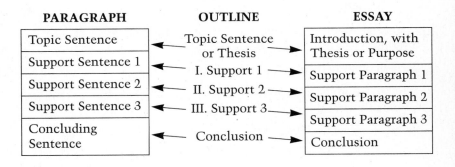

PARAGRAPH	OUTLINE	ESSAY
Topic Sentence	Topic Sentence or Thesis	Introduction, with Thesis or Purpose
Support Sentence 1	I. Support 1	Support Paragraph 1
Support Sentence 2	II. Support 2	Support Paragraph 2
Support Sentence 3	III. Support 3	Support Paragraph 3
Concluding Sentence	Conclusion	Conclusion

HANDBOOK

This handbook presents rules and examples for grammar, usage, punctuation, and capitalization. One good way to practice basic writing skills is to write your own examples. In working with verb tense, for example, you could write sentences (perhaps similar to the model sentences) in which you apply the appropriate patterns. In working with punctuation, you could write sentences that demonstrate your ability to use different punctuation marks correctly.

SUBJECTS AND VERBS

The **subject** is what the sentence is about, and the **verb** indicates what the subject is doing or is being.

Subjects

You can recognize the **simple subject** by asking Who? or What? causes the action or expresses the state of being found in the verb.

1. The **simple subject** and the **simple verb** can be single or compound.

   My *friend* and *I* have much in common.

   My friend *came* and *left* a present.

2. Although the subject usually appears before the verb, it may follow the verb.

   From tiny acorns grow mighty *oaks.*

3. The command, or **imperative,** sentence has a "you" as the implied subject, and no stated subject.

   (*You* understood) Read the notes.

4. Be careful not to confuse a subject with an **object of a preposition.**

   The *foreman* (subject) of the *jury* (object of preposition) directs discussion.

124

Verbs

Verbs show action or express being in relation to the subject.

1. **Action verbs** suggest movement or accomplishment in idea or deed.

   > He *dropped* the book. (movement)
   >
   > He *read* the book. (accomplishment)

2. **Being verbs** indicate existence.

   > They *were* concerned.

3. Verbs may appear as single words or as phrases.

   > He *led* the charge. (single word)
   >
   > She *is leading* the charge. (phrase)

4. Verbs that are joined by a coordinating conjunction such as *and* and *or* are called **compound verbs.**

   > She *worked* for twenty-five years and *retired.*

5. Do not confuse verbs with **verbals;** verbals are verblike words that function as other parts of speech.

   > The bird *singing* (participle acting as an adjective) in the tree is defending its territory.
   >
   > *Singing* (gerund acting as a noun subject) is fun.
   >
   > I want *to eat.* (infinitive acting as a noun object)

6. Do not confuse **adverbs** such as *never, not,* and *hardly* with verbs; they only modify verbs.

7. Do not overlook a part of the verb that is separated from another in a question.

   > "Where *had* the defendant *gone* on that fateful night?"

KINDS OF SENTENCES

On the basis of number and kinds of clauses, sentences may be classified as simple, compound, complex, and compound-complex.

Clauses

1. A **clause** is a group of words with a subject and a verb that functions as a part or all of a complete sentence. There are two kinds of clauses: (1) independent (main) and (2) dependent (subordinate).
2. **An independent (main) clause is a group of words with a subject and verb that can stand alone and make sense.** An independent

clause expresses a complete thought by itself and can be written as a separate sentence.

I have the money.

3. **A dependent clause, on the other hand, is a group of words with a subject and verb that depends on a main clause to give it meaning.** The dependent clause functions in the common sentence patterns as a noun, adjective, or adverb.

When I have the money

Types of Sentences

Type	Definition	Example
Simple	One independent clause	She did the work well.
Compound	Two or more independent clauses	She did the work well, and she was paid well.
Complex	One independent clause and one or more dependent clauses	*Because she did the work well*, she was paid well.
Compound-Complex	Two or more independent clauses and one or more dependent clauses	*Because she did the work well*, she was paid well, and she was satisfied.

Punctuation

1. Use a comma before a coordinating conjunction (*for, and, nor, but, or, yet, so*) between two independent clauses.

   The movie was good, but the tickets were expensive.

2. Use a comma after a dependent clause (beginning with a subordinating conjunction such as *because, although, when, since,* or *before*) that occurs before the main clause.

   When the bus arrived, we quickly boarded.

3. Use a semicolon between two independent clauses in one sentence if there is no coordinating conjunction.

   The bus arrived; we quickly boarded.

4. Use a semicolon before and usually a comma after a conjunctive adverb (such as *however, otherwise, therefore, on the other*

hand, in fact), between two independent clauses (no comma after *then, also, now, thus,* and *soon*).

> The Dodgers have not played well this year; however, the Giants have won ten games in a row.

SENTENCE PROBLEMS

Fragments

1. A correct sentence signals completeness; a **fragment** signals incompleteness—it doesn't make sense. You would expect the speaker or writer of a fragment to say or write more or to rephrase it.

2. A **dependent clause** cannot stand by itself because it begins with a subordinating word.

   > *Because* he left.
   >
   > *When* she worked.
   >
   > *Although* they slept.

3. A **verbal phrase,** a **prepositional phrase,** and an **appositive phrase** may carry ideas, but each is incomplete because it lacks a subject and verb.

   > verbal phrase: *having studied hard all evening*
   > sentence: Having studied hard all evening, John decided to retire.
   >
   > prepositional phrase: *in the store*
   > sentence: She worked in the store.
   >
   > appositive phrase: *a successful business*
   > sentence: Marks Brothers, a successful business, sells clothing.

4. Each complete sentence must have an **independent clause,** meaning a word or a group of words that contains a subject and a verb that can stand alone.

   > *He enrolled* for the fall semester.

Comma Splices and Run-Ons

1. The **comma splice** consists of two independent clauses with only a comma between them.

   > The weather was disappointing, we canceled the picnic. (A comma by itself cannot join two independent clauses.)

2. The **run-on** differs from the comma splice in only one respect: it has no comma between the independent clauses. Therefore, the run-on is two independent clauses with *nothing* between them.

> The weather was disappointing we canceled the picnic. (Independent clauses must be properly connected.)

Correcting Comma Splices and Run-Ons

1. Use a comma and a **coordinating conjunction** (*for, and, nor, but, or, yet, so*) to correct a comma splice or run-on.

> We cancelled the picnic, *for* the weather was disappointing.

2. Use a **subordinating conjunction** (such as *because, after, that, when, although, since, how, until, unless, before*) to make one clause dependent to correct a comma splice or run-on.

> *Because* the weather was disappointing, we canceled the picnic.

3. Use a **semicolon** (with or without a conjunctive adverb such as *however, otherwise, therefore, similarly, hence, on the other hand, then, consequently, also, thus*) to correct a comma splice or run-on.

> The weather was disappointing; we canceled the picnic.

> The weather was disappointing; *therefore*, we canceled the picnic.

4. Make each clause a separate sentence. For a comma splice, replace the comma with a period, and begin the second sentence (clause) with a capital letter. For a run-on, insert a period between the two independent clauses and begin the second sentence with a capital letter.

> The weather was disappointing. We canceled the picnic.

SENTENCE COMBINING

Coordination

If you intend to communicate two equally important and closely related ideas, you certainly will want to place them close together, probably in a **compound sentence** (two or more independent clauses).

1. When you combine two sentences by using a **coordinating conjunction,** drop the period, change the capital letter to a small letter, and insert a comma before the coordinating conjunction.

> I like your home, but I can visit for only three months.

2. When you combine two sentences by using a **semicolon,** replace the period with a semicolon and change the capital letter to a small letter. If you wish to use a conjunctive adverb, insert it after the semicolon and usually put a comma after it.

> I like your home. I can visit for only three months.
>
> I like your home; I can visit for only three months.
>
> I like your home; however, I can visit for only three months.

Subordination

If you have two ideas that are closely related, but one is secondary or dependent on the other, you may want to use a **complex sentence.**

> My neighbors are considerate. They never play loud music.
>
> Because my neighbors are considerate, they never play loud music.

1. If the dependent clause comes before the main clause, set it off with a comma.

> Before you dive, be sure there is water in the pool.

2. If the dependent clause comes after the main clause, set it off with a comma only if you use the word *though* or *although,* or if the words are not necessary to convey the basic meaning in the sentence.

> Be sure there is water in the pool before you dive.

Coordination and Subordination

At times you may want to show the relationship of three or more ideas within one sentence. If that relationship involves two or more main ideas and one or more supporting ideas, the combination can be stated in a **compound-complex sentence** (two or more independent clauses and one or more dependent clauses).

> Before he learned how to operate a word processor, he had trouble with his typewritten assignments, but now he produces clean, attractive material.

Use punctuation consistent with that of the compound and complex sentences.

Other Methods of Combining Ideas

1. Simple sentences can often be combined by using a prepositional phrase.

   > Dolly Parton wrote a song about a coat. The coat had many colors.
   >
   > Dolly Parton wrote a song about a coat *of many colors* (prepositional phrase).

2. To combine simple sentences, use an appositive, a noun phrase that immediately follows a noun or pronoun and renames it.

   > Susan is the leading scorer on the team. Susan is a quick and strong player.
   >
   > Susan, *a quick and strong player*, is the leading scorer on the team.

3. Simple sentences can often be combined by dropping a repeated subject in the second sentence.

   > Some items are too damaged for recycling. They must be disposed of.
   >
   > Some items are too damaged for recycling and must be disposed of.

4. Use a participial phrase, a group of words that include a participle which is a verbal that usually ends in *-ing* or *-ed*.

   > John rowed smoothly. He reached the shore.
   >
   > *Rowing smoothly*, John reached the shore.

PARALLEL STRUCTURE

1. Parallelism means balancing one structure with another of the same kind—nouns with nouns, verbs with verbs, adjectives (words that can describe nouns) with adjectives, adverbs (words that can describe verbs) with adverbs, and so forth.

   > *Men, women,* and *children* (nouns) *enjoy* the show and *return* (verbs) each year.
   >
   > She fell *in love* and *out of love* (phrases) in a few seconds.
   >
   > *She fell in love with him*, and *he fell in love with her* (clauses).

2. Faulty parallel structure is awkward and draws unfavorable attention to what is being said.

   > *To talk* with his buddies and *eating* fast foods were his favorite pastimes (should be *Talking . . . and eating* or *To talk . . . and to eat*).

3. Some words signal parallel structure. All coordinating conjunctions (*for, and, nor, but, or, yet, so*) can give such signals.

> The weather is hot *and* humid.
>
> He purchased a Dodger Dog, *but* I chose Stadium Peanuts.

4. Combination words also signal the need for parallelism or balance. The most common ones are *either/or, neither/nor, not only/but also, both/and, whether/or.*

> We will *either* win this game *or* go out fighting (verb following each of the combination words).

VERBS

The twelve verb tenses are shown below. The irregular verb *drive* is used as the example. (See page 133 for irregular verbs.)

Simple Tenses

PRESENT
I, we, you, they *drive.*
He, she, it *drives.*

Present, may imply a continuation from past to future

PAST
I, we, you, he, she, it, they *drove.*

Past

FUTURE
I, we, you, he, she, it, they *will drive.*

Future

Perfect Tenses

PRESENT PERFECT
I, we, you, they *have driven.*
He, she, it *has driven.*

Completed recently in past, may continue to present

PAST PERFECT
I, we, you, he, she, it, they *had driven.*

Prior to a specific time in the past

FUTURE PERFECT
I, we, you, he, she, it, they *will have driven.*

At a time prior to a specific time in the future

Progressive Tenses

PRESENT PROGRESSIVE
I *am driving.*
He, she, it *is driving.*   In progress now
We, you, they *are driving.*

PAST PROGRESSIVE
I, he, she, it *was driving.*   In progress in the
We, you,they *were driving.*   past

FUTURE PROGRESSIVE
I, we, you, he, she, it, they *will be*   In progress in the
driving.   future

Perfect Progressive Tenses

PRESENT PERFECT PROGRESSIVE
I, we, you, they *have been*   In progress before
driving.   now or up to now
He, she, it *has been driving.*

PAST PERFECT PROGRESSIVE
I, we, you, he, she, it, they *had been*   In progress before
driving.   another event in the
                                             past

FUTURE PERFECT PROGRESSIVE
I, we, you, he, she, it, they *will*   In progress before
have been driving.   another event in the
                                             future

Past Participles

The past participle uses the helping verbs *has, have,* or *had* along with the past tense of the verb. For regular verbs, whose past tense ends in *-ed,* the past participle form of the verb is the same as the past tense.

Below is a list of some common regular verbs, showing the base form, the past tense, and the past participle. (The base form can also be used with such helping verbs as *can, could, do, does, did, may, might, must, shall, should, will,* and *would.*)

Regular Verbs

Base Form (Present)	Past	Past Participle
ask	asked	asked
answer	answered	answered
cry	cried	cried
decide	decided	decided
dive	dived (dove)	dived
finish	finished	finished
happen	happened	happened
learn	learned	learned
like	liked	liked
love	loved	loved
need	needed	needed
open	opened	opened
start	started	started
suppose	supposed	supposed
walk	walked	walked
want	wanted	wanted

Whereas **regular verbs** are predictable—having an *-ed* ending for past and past-participle forms—**irregular verbs,** as the term suggests, follow no definite pattern.

Below is a list of some common irregular verbs, showing the base form (present), the past tense, and the past participle.

Irregular Verbs

Base Form (Present)	Past	Past Participle
arise	arose	arisen
awake	awoke (awaked)	awaked
be	was, were	been
become	became	become
begin	began	begun
bend	bent	bent
blow	blew	blown
break	broke	broken
bring	brought	brought
buy	bought	bought

Base Form (Present)	Past	Past Participle
catch	caught	caught
choose	chose	chosen
cling	clung	clung
come	came	come
creep	crept	crept
deal	dealt	dealt
do	did	done
drink	drank	drunk
drive	drove	driven
eat	ate	eaten
feel	felt	felt
fight	fought	fought
fling	flung	flung
fly	flew	flown
forget	forgot	forgotten
freeze	froze	frozen
get	got	got (gotten)
go	went	gone
grow	grew	grown
have	had	had
know	knew	known
lead	led	led
leave	left	left
lose	lost	lost
mean	meant	meant
read	read	read
ride	rode	ridden
ring	rang	rung
shine	shone	shone
shoot	shot	shot
sing	sang	sung
sink	sank	sunk
sleep	slept	slept
slink	slunk	slunk
speak	spoke	spoken
spend	spent	spent
steal	stole	stolen
stink	stank (stunk)	stunk
sweep	swept	swept
swim	swam	swum
swing	swung	swung

Base Form (Present)	Past	Past Participle
take	took	taken
teach	taught	taught
tear	tore	torn
think	thought	thought
throw	threw	thrown
wake	woke (waked)	woken (waked)
weep	wept	wept
write	wrote	written

"Problem" Verbs

The following pairs of verbs are especially troublesome and confusing: *lie* and *lay, sit* and *set,* and *rise* and *raise.* One way to tell them apart is to remember which word in each pair takes a direct object. A direct object answers the question *whom* or *what* in connection with a verb. The words *lay, raise,* and *set* take a direct object.

> He *raised* the window. (He *raised* what?)

Lie, rise, and *sit,* however, cannot take a direct object. We cannot, for example, say "He rose the window." In the examples, the italicized words are objects.

Present Tense	Meaning	Past Tense	Past Participle	Example
lie	to rest	lay	lain	I lay down to rest.
lay	to place something	laid	laid	We laid the *books* on the table.
rise	to go up	rose	risen	The smoke rose quickly.
raise	to lift	raised	raised	She raised the *question.*
sit	to rest	sat	sat	He sat in the chair.
set	to place something	set	set	They set the *basket* on the floor.

Verb Tense

These rules about selecting a **tense** for certain kinds of writing are flexible, but you should be consistent, changing tense only for a good reason.

Usually you should select the present tense to write about literature.

> Moby Dick *is* a famous white whale.

Select the past tense to write about yourself (usually) or something historical (always).

> I *was* eighteen when I *decided* I *was* ready for independence.

Subject-Verb Agreement

The basic principle of **subject-verb agreement** of number is that if the subject is singular, the verb should be singular, and if the subject is plural, the verb should be plural.

> The *advantages* of that shoe *are* obvious.
>
> There *are* many *reasons* for his poor work.
>
> The *coach,* along with the players, *protests* the decision.
>
> The *price* of those shoes *is* too high.

Voice

The **active voice** (subject, active verb, and object) is usually preferred over the **passive voice** (subject as the receiver of action, with doer unstated or at the end of a prepositional phrase).

> She read the book. (active)
>
> The book was read by her. (passive)

PRONOUNS

A pronoun is a word that is used in place of a noun.

1. **Case** is the form a pronoun takes as it fills a position in a sentence.
2. **Subjective pronouns** are *I, he,* and *she* (singular), and *we* and *they* (plural). *Who* can be either singular or plural.
   Subject case pronouns can fill subject positions.

> *We* dance in the park.
>
> It was *she* who spoke. (referring back to and meaning the same as the subject)

3. **Objective case pronouns** are *me, him,* and *her* (singular); and *us* and *them* (plural). *Whom* can be either singular or plural.
    Objective case pronouns fill object positions.

    > We saw *her* in the library. (object of verb)
    >
    > They gave the results to *us*—Judy and *me*. (object of a preposition)

4. Three techniques are useful for deciding what pronoun case to use.
    a. If you have a compound element (such as a subject or object of a preposition), consider only the pronoun part.

    > They will visit Jim and (I, me). (Consider: They will visit me.)

    b. If the next important word after *who* or *whom* in a statement is a noun or pronoun, the word choice will be *whom*; otherwise, it will be *who*. Disregard qualifier clauses such as *It seems* and *I feel*.

    > The person *who* works hardest will win.
    >
    > The person *whom* judges like will win.
    >
    > The person *who*, we think, worked hardest won. (ignoring the qualifier clause)

    c. *Let's* is made up of the words *let* and *us* and means *"you let us"*; therefore, when you select a pronoun to follow it, consider the two original words and select another object word—*me*.

    > Let's you and *me* go to town.

5. A **pronoun** agrees with its antecedent in person, number, and gender.
    a. Avoid needless shifting in **person,** which means shifting in point of view, such as from *I* to *you*.

    > *I* tried but *you* couldn't persuade her to return. (incorrect)
    >
    > *I* tried but *I* couldn't persuade her to return. (correct)

    b. Most problems with pronoun-antecedent agreement involve **number.** The principles are simple: If the antecedent (the word the pronoun refers back to) is singular, use a singular pronoun. If the antecedent is plural, use a plural pronoun.

    > Jim forgot *his* notebook.
    >
    > Many students cast *their* votes today.
    >
    > Someone lost *his* or *her* (not *their*) book.

c. The pronoun should agree with its antecedent in **gender,** if the gender of the antecedent is specific. Masculine and feminine pronouns are gender-specific: *he, him, she, her.* Others are neuter: *I, we, me, us, it, they, them, who, whom, that, which.* The words *who* and *whom* refer to people. *That* can refer to ideas, things, and people, but usually not to people. *Which* refers to ideas and things, but never to people. In order to avoid a perceived sex bias, most writers and speakers prefer to use *he or she* or *his or her* instead of just *he* or *his;* however many writers simply make antecedents plural.

> Everyone should work until *he* or *she* drops.

> People should work until *they* drop.

ADJECTIVES AND ADVERBS

1. **Adjectives** modify (describe) nouns and pronouns and answer the questions *Which one? What kind?* and *How many?*
2. **Adverbs** modify verbs, adjectives, or other adverbs and answer the questions *Where? When? Why?* and *How?* Most words ending in *-ly* are adverbs.
3. If you settle for a common word such as *good* or a slang word such as *neat* to characterize something you like, you will be limiting your communication. The more precise the word, the better the communication. Keep in mind, however, that anything can be overdone; therefore, use adjectives and adverbs wisely and economically.
4. For making comparisons, most adjectives and adverbs have three different forms: the positive (one), the comparative (two), and the superlative (three or more).
   a. Adjectives
      1. Add an *-er* to short adjectives (one or two syllables) to rank units of two.

         > Julian is *kinder* than Sam.

      2. Add an *-est* to short adjectives (one or two syllables) to rank units of more than two.

         > Of the fifty people I know, Julian is the *kindest.*

      3. Add the word *more* to long adjectives to rank units of two.

         > My hometown is *more beautiful* than yours.

4. Add the word *most* to long adjectives to rank units of three or more.

   My hometown is the *most beautiful* in all America.

5. Some adjectives are irregular in the way they change to show comparison.

   good, better, best; bad, worse, worst

b. Adverbs
   For most adverbs, use the word *more* before the comparative form (two) and the word *most* before the superlative form (three or more).

   Jim performed *skillfully*. (modifier)

   Joan performed *more skillfully* (comparative modifier) than Joan.

   But Susan performed *most skillfully* (superlative modifier) of all.

5. **Avoid double negatives.** Words such as *no, not, none, nothing, never, hardly, barely,* and *scarcely* should not be combined.

   I *don't* have *no* time for recreation. (incorrect)

   I have no time for recreation. (correct)

   I don't have time for recreation. (correct)

6. Do not confuse adjectives (*bad*) with adverbs (*badly*).
7. A modifier that gives information but doesn't refer to a word already in the sentence is called a **dangling modifier.**

   Walking down the street, a snake startled me. (dangling)

   Walking down the street, I was startled by a snake. (correct)

8. A modifier that is placed so that it modifies the wrong word or words is called a **misplaced modifier.**

   The sick man went to a doctor *with a high fever*. (misplaced)

   The sick man with a high fever went to a doctor. (correct)

PUNCTUATION

1. The three marks of end punctuation are periods, question marks, and exclamation points.
   a. Periods
      Place a period after a statement.
      Place a period after common abbreviations.

b. Question Marks
Place a **question mark** at the end of a direct question.
Use a single question mark in sentence constructions that contain a double question—that is, a quoted question following a question.

> Mr. Martin said, "Did he say, 'Are we going?'"

Do *not* use a question mark after an indirect (reported) question.

> She asked me what caused the slide.

c. Exclamation Points
Place an **exclamation point** after a word or group of words that expresses strong feeling.
Do not overwork the exclamation point. Do not use double exclamation points.

2. The **comma** is used essentially to separate and to set off sentence elements.

a. Use a comma to separate main clauses joined by one of the coordinating conjunctions—*for, and, nor, but, or, yet, so.*

> We went to the game, *but* it was canceled.

b. Use a comma after introductory dependent clauses and long phrases (generally, four or more words is considered long).

> *Before she and I arrived,* the meeting was called to order.

c. Use a comma to separate words, phrases, and clauses in a series.

> He ran *down the street, across the park,* and into the arms of his father.

d. Use a comma to separate coordinate adjectives not joined by *and* that modify the same noun.

> I need a *sturdy, reliable* truck.

e. Use a comma to separate sentence elements that might be misread.

> Inside, the dog scratched his fleas.

f. Use commas to set off nonessential (unnecessary for meaning of the sentence) words, phrases, and clauses.

> Maria, who studied hard, will pass.

g. Use commas to set off nouns used as direct address.

> Play it again, Sam.

h. Use commas to separate the numbers in a date.

> June 4, 1965, is a day I will remember.

i. Use commas to separate the city from the state. No comma is used between the state and the ZIP code.

> Walnut, CA 91789

j. Use a comma following the salutation and the complementary closing in a letter (but in a business letter, use a colon after the salutation).

> Dear John,
>
> Sincerely,

k. Use a comma in numbers to set off groups of three digits. However, omit the comma in dates and in long serial numbers, page numbers, and street numbers.

> The total assets were $2,000,000.
>
> I was born in 1980.

3. The semicolon indicates a stronger division than the comma. It is used principally to separate independent clauses within a sentence.

a. Use a semicolon to separate independent clauses not joined by a coordinating conjunction.

> You must buy that car today; tomorrow will be too late.

b. Use a semicolon between two independent clauses joined by a conjunctive adverb (such as *however, otherwise, therefore, similarly, hence, on the other hand, then, consequently, accordingly, thus*).

> It was very late; therefore, I remained at the hotel.

4. Quotation marks bring special attention to words.

a. Quotation marks are used principally to set off direct quotations. A direct quotation consists of material taken from the written work or the direct speech of others; it is set off by double quotation marks. Single quotation marks are used to set off a quotation within a quotation.

> He said, "I don't remember if she said, 'Wait for me.'"

b. Use double quotation marks to set off titles of shorter pieces of writing such as magazine articles, essays, short stories, short poems, one-act plays, chapters in books, songs, and separate pieces of writing published as part of a larger work.

> The book *Literature: Structure, Sound, and Sense* contains a deeply moving poem entitled "On Wenlock Edge."
>
> Have you read "The Use of Force," a short story by William Carlos Williams?
>
> My favorite Elvis song is "Don't Be Cruel."

c. Punctuation with quotation marks follows definite rules.
   1. A period or comma is always placed *inside* the quotation marks.

> Our assignment for Monday was to read Poe's "The Raven."
>
> "I will read you the story," he said. "It is a good one."

   2. A semicolon or colon is always placed *outside* the quotation marks.

> He read Robert Frost's poem "Design"; then he gave the examination.

   3. A question mark, exclamation point, or dash is placed *outside* the quotation marks when it applies to the entire sentence and *inside* the quotation marks when it applies to the material in quotation marks.

> He asked, "Am I responsible for everything?" (quoted question within a statement)
>
> Did you hear him say, "I have the answer"? (statement within a question)
>
> Did she say, "Are we ready?" (question within a question)
>
> She shouted, "Impossible!" (exclamation)
>
> "I hope—that is, I—" he began. (dash)

5. Italics (slanting type) is used to call special attention to certain words or groups of words. In handwriting or typing, such words are <u>underlined</u>.
   a. Italicize (underline) foreign words and phrases that are still listed in the dictionary as foreign.

> *nouveau riche   Weltschmerz*

b. Italicize (underline) titles of books (except the Bible), long poems, plays, magazines, motion pictures, musical compositions, newspapers, works of art, names of aircraft, ships, and letters, figures, and words referred to by their own name.

> *War and Peace*   *Apollo 12*   leaving *o* out of *sophomore*

6. The dash is used when a stronger break than the comma is needed. It can also be used to indicate a break in the flow of thought and to emphasize words (less formal than the colon in this situation).

> Here is the true reason—but maybe you don't care.
>
> English, French, history—these are the subjects I like.

7. The colon is a formal mark of punctuation used chiefly to introduce something that is to follow, such as a list, a quotation, or an explanation.

> These cars are my favorites: Cadillac, Chevrolet, Buick, Oldsmobile, and Pontiac.

8. Parentheses are used to set off material that is of relatively little importance to the main thought of the sentence. Such material—numbers, parenthetical material, figures, supplementary material, and sometimes explanatory details—merely amplifies the main thought.

> The years of the era (1961–1973) were full of action.
>
> Her husband (she had been married only a year) died last week.

9. Brackets are used within a quotation to set off editorial additions or corrections made by the person who is quoting.

> Churchill said: "It [the Yalta Agreement] contained many mistakes."

10. The apostrophe is used with nouns and indefinite pronouns to show possession, to show the omission of letters and figures in contractions, and to form the plurals of letters, figures, and words referred to as words.

> man's coat, girls' clothes, *you're* (contraction of *you are*), five *and's*

11. The hyphen brings two or more words together into a single compound word. Correct hyphenation, therefore, is essentially a spelling problem rather than one of punctuation. Because the

hyphen is not used with any degree of consistency, consult your dictionary for current usage. Study the following as a beginning guide.

a. Use a hyphen to separate the parts of many compound words.

> about-face, go-between

b. Use a hyphen between prefixes and proper names.

> all-American, mid-November

c. Use a hyphen to join two or more words used as a single adjective modifier before a noun.

> first-class service, hard-fought game, sad-looking mother

d. Use a hyphen with spelled-out compound numbers up to ninety-nine and with fractions.

> twenty-six, two-thirds

Note: Dates, street addresses, numbers requiring more than two words, chapter and page numbers, time followed directly by *a.m.* or *p.m.*, and figures after a dollar sign or before measurement abbreviations are usually written as figures, not words.

CAPITALIZATION

In English, there are many conventions concerning the use of capital letters. Here are some of them.

1. Capitalize the first word of a sentence.
2. Capitalize proper nouns and adjectives derived from proper nouns.

Names of persons:

Edward Jones

Adjectives derived from proper nouns:

a Shakespearean sonnet, a Miltonic sonnet

Countries, nationalities, races, languages:

Germany, English, Spanish, Chinese

States, regions, localities, other geographical divisions:

California, the Far East, the South

Oceans, lakes, mountains, deserts, streets, parks:

Lake Superior, Fifth Avenue, Sahara Desert

Educational institutions, schools, courses:

Santa Ana College, Spanish 3, Joe Hill School, Rowland High School

Organizations and their members:

Boston Red Sox, Boy Scouts, Audubon Society

Corporations, governmental agencies or departments, trade names:

U.S. Steel Corporation, Treasury Department, White Memorial Library

Calendar references such as holidays, days of the week, months:

Easter, Tuesday, January

Historic eras, periods, documents, laws:

Declaration of Independence, Geneva Convention, First Crusade, Romantic Age

3. Capitalize words denoting family relationships when they are used before a name or substituted for a name.

> He walked with his nephew and Aunt Grace.
>
> but
>
> He walked with his nephew and his aunt.
>
> Grandmother and Mother are away on vacation.
>
> but
>
> My grandmother and my mother are away on vacation.

4. Capitalize abbreviations after names.

> Henry White, Jr.
>
> William Green, M.D.

5. Capitalize titles of themes, books, plays, movies, poems, magazines, newspapers, musical compositions, songs, and works of art. Do not capitalize short conjunctions and prepositions unless they come at the beginning or the end of the title.

> *Desire Under the Elms*   *Terminator*
>
> *Last of the Mohicans*   *Of Mice and Men*
>
> "Blueberry Hill"

6. Capitalize any title preceding a name or used as a substitute for a name. Do not capitalize a title following a name.

Judge Stone	Alfred Stone, a judge
General Clark	Raymond Clark, a general
Professor Fuentes	Harry Jones, the former president

INDEX